THE BLIND ADVANTAGE

*How Going Blind Made Me a
Stronger Principal and How Including
Children with Disabilities Made Our
School Better for Everyone*

BILL HENDERSON

Ch. 5-7

Harvard Education Press
Cambridge, Massachusetts

Third Printing, 2018

Library of Congress Control Number 2011928652

Paperback ISBN 978-1-61250-109-3
Library Edition ISBN 978-1-61250-110-9

Published by Harvard Education Press,
an imprint of the Harvard Education Publishing Group

Harvard Education Press
8 Story Street
Cambridge, MA 02138

Cover photograph by Marc Yankus.
Cover design by Sarah Henderson.

The typefaces used in this book are Legacy Serif ITC and Knockout.

*I am very grateful to the many champions of
inclusion whom I encountered while I was privileged
to be principal of the O'Hearn Elementary School.
This book is dedicated to them.*

CONTENTS

ACKNOWLEDGMENTS
vii

INTRODUCTION
1

CHAPTER 1
Journey Toward the Light
9

CHAPTER 2
*Determination:
Inclusion Will Work*
27

CHAPTER 3
*Vision: A Multi-Abled Learning Community
with Many Paths Toward Success*
43

CHAPTER 4
Sensitivity with High Expectations
65

CHAPTER 5

Organization and Planning for Success

79

CHAPTER 6

Collaboration Among Staff

97

CHAPTER 7

Collaboration with Students

113

CHAPTER 8

Collaboration with Families

125

CHAPTER 9

Collaboration with Outside Supporters

147

CHAPTER 10

Humor, Levity, and Grace

167

EPILOGUE

185

ABOUT THE AUTHOR

191

ACKNOWLEDGMENTS

Without the students, staff, parents, and other supporters of the O'Hearn, there would be no story for me to tell.

Without family, friends, and allies in the disability community, I would not have the fortitude to tell it.

Without the Harvard Education Press editor, Caroline Chauncey, this book would not have come together in the same way.

Without my wife, Margie, this story and so much of what has been special in my life would not have happened.

All proceeds from the sale of this book will be dedicated to support inclusion at the Henderson Inclusion School.

INTRODUCTION

It was 8:55 a.m. on a sunny October day. The doors would be opening soon for another day of learning at the O'Hearn Elementary School in Boston. As the principal, I needed to start my regular morning check-in routine. I excused myself from a before-school discussion with third-, fourth-, and fifth-grade teachers on solving complex math problems, facilitated by a university professor. As I left the auditorium and headed toward the back entrance to greet students, a teacher came up alongside me and raised some concerns regarding techniques used by a therapist with one of her students. Further down the corridor, another staff member stopped me to inform me that she might have to leave early to take her sick daughter to the doctor.

Outside, by the back yard area, where children and families were gathering before it was time to enter, I intervened with a small group of students who were arguing about whether a boy was "out" or "safe" in their before-school kickball game. A paraprofessional on morning duty handed me a disciplinary report from a bus driver about a student who had thrown a pencil out the window on the way to school. A steady stream of students and parents came over to say hello or to ask a variety questions, and one girl proudly showed off how she maneuvered her new electric wheelchair.

Inside the building, right after the morning bell rang, I called back some students I heard running down the corridor as they tried to be first in line for breakfast. On my way to the cafeteria, I greeted the kindergarten teachers and checked on a few issues with them. A substitute teacher approached me and asked for clarification about her schedule. I stopped for a few moments to chat with some parents and children who were admiring some artwork outside a classroom.

When I entered the breakfast area, the cafeteria attendant called me over and pointed out some possible mouse droppings. Students at a nearby table became noisy because somebody had knocked over another student's cereal, which was now dripping onto the floor. The custodian was out sick that day, and there would be no replacement for at least a few hours, so the nurse and I grabbed some paper towels and got a couple of kids to clean it up. A mother approached me to tell me that she felt her son had received an unfair grade on his report card. Another parent proudly voiced that she hoped that her daughter, who had been struggling with reading and writing, could show me her essay, which had been selected for the exemplar bulletin board.

As I hurried toward the main office, a teacher shouted out how a student had lost her social studies book and that there were no extras in the storage closet. Some fifth grade girls approached me and excitedly described their roles in the upcoming school play. A therapist coming out of the restroom pointed out that the nearby water container was empty, so I quickly put on another five-gallon bottle. I heard the one beep from the intercom system, which was a signal from the school secretary for me to contact the office and which probably meant that my ride to go to the principals' meeting had arrived.

Back near the front door, a father who seldom visited the school approached me and told me that he needed to have a serious conversation with me about a boy who he believed had bothered his autistic and mostly nonverbal son while the boys were in the bathroom the previous day. I expressed my regrets and assured him that the teachers would monitor the situation closely and that I would investigate and contact him later that same afternoon. I quickly shared the father's concerns with the teacher who would be covering for me while I was out of the building and reminded her of a couple of points to make during morning announcements. Then I shouted good-bye to those standing by the office and hustled outside to my colleague, who was waiting to drive us to the principals' meeting.

All of these interactions had occurred in less than twenty minutes before classes had even begun. As the principal and as the school's only administrator, I was primarily responsible for dealing with that morning's issues and with the many others that would arise daily from the 240 students, fifty-five full and part-time staff, hundreds of parents and extended family members, and many supporters from local universities and agencies.

This morning scenario was typical. It will sound familiar to most principals and particularly to those who are the only administrator in their buildings. Unlike most principals, though, I am blind. Some principals might assume that they couldn't handle a job like this if they were blind. And in fact, over the years, a number of people had told me just that.

Reflecting on my twenty years at the O'Hearn, I recognize that although being blind did pose some challenges, it did not hinder

3

me from the essential aspects of my work as a principal. In fact, in some ways, blindness created some opportunities for me.

During the twenty-minute morning scenario I just described, there were relatively few additional efforts because of my blindness. Before leaving for the principals' meeting, I did have to ask a colleague for a ride. During my check-in routine, I asked some students whose voices I had not recognized to identify themselves. After returning to the school from the principals' meeting, I asked the teacher whose student had thrown the pencil out the school bus window to review the disciplinary report orally with me. I also asked the girl whose mother wanted me to see her essay on the exemplar bulletin board to come out of her room and to read it out loud to me.

These extra efforts related to my blindness were not a big deal, and I actually feel that I benefitted from the opportunity of having to connect with and communicate more with the teacher, students, and principal colleague who helped me. Frankly, the extra time that I spent on those tasks due to blindness paled in comparison with all the other work that I needed to do to address the other issues that had arisen in those twenty minutes of that particular morning.

Over the years, there were indeed ways that blindness made my work as principal more complicated, and I will refer to some of these challenges throughout this book. Upon reflection, though, I also have to acknowledge how going blind had a positive impact on me and ultimately helped prepare me to be a more effective principal for the O'Hearn. Living with blindness forced me to learn how to deal with many issues creatively and differently, and I gained a unique perspective on disability and inclusion. Inclusion was clearly a personal struggle for me long before it became a professional responsibility. Figuring out how to keep working as a blind educator helped me to further develop important qualities that affected how I functioned as a person and a principal.

In the upcoming chapters, I will offer a brief introduction to myself and the school and will describe how the experience of losing my sight helped me to develop and strengthen the following key qualities: determination, vision, sensitivity, organization, collaboration, and humor. These important characteristics have relevance for all school leaders and were certainly critical in helping me become a stronger principal of an inclusive school. I will also highlight and share many anecdotes that show how some of these same qualities were demonstrated by students with disabilities themselves, and how these qualities elicited positive responses from others.

The remaining chapters in this book discuss these six key qualities and are divided into sections that present students' challenges, my challenges as a principal, and school implications. These stories are intertwined. While I was figuring out how to function as a principal who was also blind, and while I and the rest of the school community were trying to figure out how to include students with a range of abilities, we had to develop a school where all students could learn and succeed. This was a journey of discovery for me personally and for the school community.

The book includes four chapters on collaboration: collaboration with staff, among students, with families, and with external supporters. This emphasis reflects the special role that collaboration played at the O'Hearn. Every effective school requires the cooperation and contributions of all its stakeholders. Inclusion accentuates the need for more extensive collaboration and makes its potential far more powerful. For instance, while no principal is omniscient, blindness probably forced me to utilize collaboration more than my sighted counterparts would have used it. There was no pretense that I alone could control everything that occurred in our school. Having so many students with disabilities at the O'Hearn also forced the entire school community to collaborate more. Together we came to recognize that even though we sometimes needed help, there were ways that all of us could be helpful.

Helping children learn and succeed in inclusive classrooms requires talents and skills that need to be developed continuously in order to improve teaching and learning. Equally important to this expertise is the ability to relate to, and work with, others. Positive beliefs and attitudes about those who have disabilities are critical. Throughout this book, I celebrate the contributions of many individuals who, through their daily words and actions at the O'Hearn, made inclusion happen. Most of these champions of inclusion would say that what they did was quite ordinary and no big deal. What was extraordinary about them, though, was that they demonstrated on a regular basis how ordinary it could be for students with and without disabilities to learn together and succeed.

Except for background information, the situations in this book are based on experiences that occurred at the O'Hearn between 1989 and 2009. Most of the anecdotes involving students focus on children who have disabilities, even though, as a group, they represented only about one-third of the total student population. Students without disabilities were indeed an integral part of the O'Hearn community, and inclusive education could not have thrived without them and without their strong participation and achievement. Good inclusion requires effective general education.

This book's focus on disabilities is intentional, though. Disability is sometimes viewed as a negative phenomenon. Impairments or disorders in and of themselves are, of course, not conditions that most would choose. However, the process and outcomes of dealing with disabilities and disorders can be positive and rewarding to many. I now recognize that the blindness that I had initially feared actually helped me develop leadership abilities. Likewise, the inclusion of children with disabilities at the O'Hearn—a step that some people had doubted could be successful—ultimately helped the school community develop into a more effective learning environment for everyone.

Most important, including students with a range of disabilities became the catalyst for the transformation of general education at our school. Students who have disabilities, and particularly those with significant challenges, are often blamed for lowering standards and performance in schools. On the contrary, their inclusion at the O'Hearn helped us figure out how to improve teaching and learning for everyone. I hope that the readers of this book will become more aware of the potential of persons with disabilities and will be better equipped to promote inclusion in their own learning communities.

Note: Throughout this book, all names of students and some details of their specific circumstances have been altered to protect the rights and privacy of children.

1

◈

JOURNEY TOWARD THE LIGHT

THE DARKENING

"You should get out of education."

This was the recommendation thrust upon me in 1974 by a leading eye specialist. I was twenty-four and had just finished participating in a full day of eye exams using new equipment and tests at a highly regarded medical center in Boston. My wife, Margie, and I were meeting with the doctor in his office. I had first been diagnosed with RP (retinitis pigmentosa) when I was twelve. However, up until then, the degenerative eye disease had posed only relatively minor visual challenges for me, primarily at night or in other darkened situations, and I had been told that my eyesight was not going to deteriorate significantly until I reached my sixties. When I met with this retina specialist, I had just completed my first year of teaching at a Boston middle school. The doctor explained how his examination indicated I would probably lose most of my functional vision in the next five to fifteen years. I was shocked and speechless. He questioned me about what I did for work. I mumbled that I was a teacher. When he asked me if I liked my work, I replied that most of the time, I did. Then he jolted me with his devastating pronouncement: "You should get out of education."

Leaving the doctor's office, I felt dazed. I did not believe that this could be happening to me. I kept telling myself that I could not lose my vision while I was still young and that I should not have to leave a career that I enjoyed. So I dismissed and even denied what the doctor had just told me. I worked hard to convince myself that the doctor was a total jerk and that he had no clue what he was talking about.

In time, the doctor's words would prove to be half right. He responsibly communicated what he determined to be the physical realities of my vision loss. However, he was wrong when he irresponsibly communicated his ignorance of human possibilities. Looking back on that day, I realize that the doctor also failed miserably by sending me off to navigate a transition to a darkening world without any direction or support except for the recommendation that I have a follow-up eye exam in a year's time.

As I clung to the hope that my eyesight would remain the same, my life following that doctor's visit was certainly full of activities. Between 1976 and 1979, my wife and I became parents of three children, Meg, Tony, and Joya. I was very involved with raising our children and spent lots of time playing with them end enjoyed being a dad. Professionally, I continued teaching English, Spanish, and social studies to middle school students. I also coached soccer and track teams. I volunteered for various service organizations in my community. In addition to these activities, I cultivated and helped maintain a neighborhood garden as well as my own vegetable garden. While busy doing all of these things, I also took graduate courses and earned a master's degree in education.

In spite of these activities, as I neared the age of thirty, I had to admit—and another eye specialist confirmed—that my vision was getting worse. Because the spots on my retinas were getting bigger, my peripheral field was getting smaller and my capacity to discern fine details was worsening. I started feeling eyestrain while reading print that was fuzzy or faded. I sometimes had to ask my students to change their pens or to press down harder on their pencils when they were completing written assignments. I bumped into people and objects more frequently while moving around quickly in crowded areas. This caused me much embarrassment as well as some bruises. It took me longer to locate items that I had dropped or that had been moved, and this was frustrating. I wisely let my driver's license expire, but I missed the flexibility and freedom that driving affords. At times, being able to still see a great deal while simultaneously dealing with increased vision loss was awkward for me. Basically, around most people except my family and closest friends, I tried hard to pretend that my vision was normal, but this was becoming increasingly difficult to pull off.

I was getting worried, and I wasn't sure what I was going to do. I decided to seek advice, but this time, it wouldn't be with a medical doctor who didn't know much about me or the work that I was doing. I scheduled an appointment with a local education leader who knew about my teaching and about some of my involvement in school activities. He had previously praised me for facilitating the integration of Hispanic students and for coordinating a drop-out prevention program at the middle school where I taught. I shared with the administrator how

I had RP and that I might be losing most of my vision. He expressed his surprise and regrets. Then I asked him what he thought that I, an active and successful teacher, might do if I were to become blind. He pondered for a while and then asked me how long I had been working in Boston. I responded that I was just completing my seventh year. This information seemed to perk him up, and after pausing as if he were delivering a special announcement, he declared that with that amount of time teaching, I would have no problems, since I qualified for disability retirement. His recommendation left me numb.

While I was studying at Yale University, I had presumed that I could choose any career and do just about any job that I wanted to. In addition to being a student, I had also gained valuable experience in various other areas, including landscaping, serving as a lifeguard and camp counselor, distributing earthquake relief supplies, and constructing adobe houses in Peru, studying in Mexico, and completing student teaching in the New Haven Public Schools. Upon graduation in 1972, I moved to Boston and joined a group called Casa del Sol, which was involved with community organizing in a neighborhood with many new immigrants. Because I also needed some income, I took a job unloading trucks at a nearby shoe factory. That next summer, I had the opportunity to travel again to Mexico. It was upon my return to Boston in September 1973 that I was hired as a middle school teacher.

I had never imagined that anyone would tell me to get out of education or to apply for early retirement. Given my decreasing vision and the advice that I had received, though, questions about what work I was going to be able to do started to nag me. I pondered lots of options, including teaching oral English to adult immigrants, translating between English and Spanish at local hospitals, joining a nonprofit agency that promoted development in Latin America, and picking apples and doing farm work. At one point, I even considered following the example of Ray Charles and Stevie Wonder. They were both blind, and I enjoyed their music. We purchased an old piano, and I started taking some lessons. After much practice, I was able to crank out a few tunes, but realized it definitely wasn't going to be my career. Even our loyal family dog, who usually wanted to stay by my side, tired of listening to my playing and headed to another area in the house, where he could find more peace.

I was losing my vision, and I was confused. During that time of many doubts, I was fortunate to experience the love and support from family and friends. I also maintained an underlying faith that things would eventually work out. My gut told me that what the doctor and the education leader had advised me to do—to stop teaching and to just drop out—was absurd and made no sense for someone who was just thirty years old and in good health. However, as much as I hated to admit it, I had to do something else, and I needed to start dealing with my vision loss.

THE ILLUMINATION

It was at this point that I finally connected with some real "experts." Having accepted that I needed guidance, I reached out to others who were already dealing with blindness. One self-help group for blind and visually impaired individuals, I learned, was organized by the Vision Foundation of Massachusetts. I called the number, and a friendly person invited me to attend the next meeting. That meeting was a surprise—dare I say an eye-opener?—for me. The adults who all had varying degrees of vision loss seemed, except for eyesight, pretty normal. One was a sales person, one was an administrator at a prison, one was a counselor, one repaired bicycles, one worked at a fish processing plant, one was on disability retirement, and two were back in school studying. All the adults shared their stories, including some of their joys and their challenges. Interestingly, those who had the least amount of vision seemed to be more comfortable about living with their blindness, while those of us with more vision seemed more agitated over it. These conversations were transformative in helping me recognize how blind and visually impaired individuals could be successfully involved in all aspects of life.

Subsequently, I was referred to and became a member of both the National Federation of the Blind and the American Council of the Blind. Both groups are national consumer groups representing and advocating for the blind and visually impaired. I started receiving their literature and attended meetings with their state and local affiliates around the Boston area. I admired the leadership and advocacy of these organizations and relished the connections with many members who were active and contributing in their communities and who were blind. Through these groups, I learned that there were even national associations of blind teachers and that blind professionals were successfully contributing at all levels of education.

Bolstered by these connections with the disability community, I started feeling some hope, but I knew that I still needed to better prepare myself for blindness and for future career opportunities. Because my vision had decreased to the point that I was considered legally blind, I was registered with the Massachusetts Commission for the Blind, which entitled me to receive supportive services. I enrolled with the Perkins Braille and Talking Book Library of the Blind and received access to thousands of books on discs and four-track cassettes. I quickly discovered how listening to books on cassette allowed me to greatly reduce eyestrain. Because the reading machines had features that controlled the speed of the recorded text and because I could also listen to books while engaged with household or yard work, I was also able to greatly increase the amount of material that I was reading.

Somewhat reluctantly, I scheduled lessons with a mobility instructor from the Carroll Center for the Blind. He met me at varying locations around Boston and started to teach me beginning techniques in using a white cane. Initially, I felt self-conscious and almost fraudulent about using a cane, because I could still see a lot of things. The instructor quickly showed me how I could walk much more rapidly and safely using the cane. It certainly alerted others to move out of my way, and it kept me from smashing into posts and other protruding objects.

Soon thereafter, I started taking advantage of new technologies demonstrated by experts associated with various agencies that supported the blind and visually impaired. They first recommended that I use a closed-circuit TV hooked to a computer that provided greater contrast and enlarged the print for me. But with my decreasing vision and increased use of the Internet and word processing, I eventually switched to using screen readers, which provide voice output and alternative (using keys instead of a mouse) navigation techniques. Eventually, I became accustomed to accelerating the screen reader to a speed at which I could handle my e-mail correspondence and read other documents as quickly as when I was able to read with my eyes.

I also received instruction in Braille and started using it regularly. Although my speed at reading Braille was nowhere comparable to the speed at which I listened to material, I found it to be most valuable particularly for note taking and retrieving specific data. Books with both print and Braille that I purchased from National Braille Press or borrowed from the Perkins Library certainly came in handy at school. Interestingly, I noticed that many of the individuals helping me learn new skills or offering supportive services were themselves blind. Clearly, all the persons—sighted or not—from these agencies and consumer groups serving and representing the blind and visually impaired were incredibly significant in helping prepare me technically and emotionally to continue my career and professional growth in education.

Although national legislation enacted in the 1970s prohibited dismissing or otherwise discriminating against employees because of blindness, I knew that I, a person with a disability, would still need to demonstrate how I would successfully fulfill the primary responsibilities of my job. Many colleagues within the Boston Public Schools were encouraging. In 1981, I applied for and accepted a position in curriculum development and staff training. This new opportunity led me to connect with a two-way bilingual (English and Spanish) school where I soon thereafter became assistant principal. Despite my dwindling vision, the principal and teachers there supported me as I involved myself with the complexities of administration, including the supervision of students and staff. These educators had an expectation that I "would figure it out." I was fortunate to be an administrator in a school where hard work and improvements were the norm for all and where I was able to contribute. Because I found being an assistant principal exciting and fulfilling, I decided to enroll in a part-time doctoral program in educational leadership at the University of Massachusetts in order to better prepare myself for future opportunities as an administrator.

While I was an assistant principal and finishing my doctorate, I developed some curricula and led workshops on promoting disability awareness. Federal law had been enacted requiring public schools to accept and educate students with disabilities and to consider ways of integrating these children in the least restrictive environment. Parents in Boston and in the rest of the country were educating themselves about these new rights and were lobbying for increased opportunities for their children. For any such integration to be successful, students without disabilities, as well as their teachers, would need to learn more about students with disabilities.

In 1988, as part of my promotion of disability awareness, I connected with a group of parents who were advocating that the Boston Public Schools designate a school where students with even the most significant disabilities could learn together in classrooms with their nondisabled peers. A task force of parents and educators was formed by the Boston School Department to make recommendations regarding this endeavor, and I was an active member. With this group's guidance and with tenacious lobbying by parents, the Boston School Committee voted that the Patrick O'Hearn Elementary School would start integrating children with significant disabilities in September 1989. A few weeks before the school opened, the superintendent appointed me to be the school's new principal. Having struggled to discover my own ways to stay included in education, I would now have the privilege of leading an effort to educate and integrate students with a variety of disabilities, including many who had previously been excluded from learning with their nondisabled peers.

THE PATRICK O'HEARN ELEMENTARY SCHOOL

The O'Hearn Elementary School is part of the Boston Public Schools and is located in Dorchester, a large and rather densely populated neighborhood of the city. With a rich history, the community has served as a starting point for many immigrants to this country and continues to have a wide ethnic and linguistic diversity. Some sections of Dorchester are quite poor, some are working class or lower middle class, and a few areas are considered more middle class and prosperous. Triple-decker, two-family, and single-family houses are typical, along with some apartment buildings.

The O'Hearn facility, with its brick facade, was constructed in 1957 at a busy intersection on Dorchester Avenue. Eleven classrooms are situated on three of the four corridors that run around the fairly large inner courtyard or playground; these corridors form a slightly irregular rectangle. The school also has a small cafeteria and a larger multipurpose room (used as a gymnasium, an auditorium, a meeting area, and a therapy site). Because all instruction and activities occur on the first floor (the basement being just for storage, heating, and maintenance equipment), making the building handicapped accessible was not that complex a process. The Boston School Department provided periodic renovations and regular maintenance, and the building was generally viewed as being welcoming and a good place for children to learn.

Students who attended the O'Hearn lived in what was called the East Zone section of Boston. For assignment purposes, the School Department then divided the city into three zones. Each zone was responsible for serving approximately ten thousand elementary-aged children, who could attend one of the approximately thirty elementary schools. Under Boston's Controlled Choice Student Assignment Plan, most parents could choose up to seven schools for their children to attend. Through the use of a computerized program, over 90 percent of families received one of their top three choices. If they were assigned a school that was located more than one mile from where they lived, busing was provided at no cost. Parents of children who had moderate or significant disabilities had fewer options. The Special Education Department of the Boston Public Schools designated specific schools for these children according to programmatic availability and on placement recommendations from Individualized Education Program (IEP) teams.

The O'Hearn would prove to become a wonderful example of inclusion. The 240 students came together from very diverse ethnic and linguistic backgrounds and abilities. A review of overall demographics in the twenty years that I was principal (from 1989 to 2009) indicated that approximately 45 percent of students were African American, 30 percent were Caucasian, and 25 percent were newcomers from many countries around the globe, with the highest numbers from various Caribbean islands, Vietnam, Cape Verde, Guyana, and Ireland. A majority of families at the O'Hearn qualified for free and reduced lunches based on income, but some families were considered more middle class.

Because there were not many options for inclusive education in the East Zone of Boston, and because many parents had strongly advocated for their children with disabilities to be assigned to our school, the O'Hearn had a high concentration of children with many different special needs. Approximately 33 percent of the school's overall population had one or more disabilities. Every year, the O'Hearn served many students with intellectual or developmental disabilities (or both) including relatively large numbers who had Down syndrome or who were on the autism spectrum. Many children were diagnosed with specific learning disabilities, speech impairments, or emotional disorders. Individuals who had cerebral palsy, spina bifida, osteogenesis imperfecta (brittle bones) or other health impairments, blindness or low vision, as well as individuals with multiple disabilities also attended our school. Although some students with hearing impairments were enrolled at the O'Hearn, most deaf students opted to attend the district school for the deaf, where most staff and students used sign language.

All O'Hearn students with and without disabilities learned together in inclusive classrooms from early childhood through grade five. On average, a typical class at the O'Hearn served a total of twenty-three students (usually about fifteen students without disabilities, four students with significant disabilities, and three or four students with mild or moderate disabilities).

Each O'Hearn classroom was staffed with two teachers (one with special education certification and one with elementary education certification). Most classrooms also received some part-time support from one of the school's paraprofessionals (sometimes referred to as teacher assistants or aides) who were primarily responsible for assisting multiple students with significant disabilities primarily with activities of daily living, including toileting, feeding, and completion of basic tasks. There were also typically over ten therapists who worked at the school on a part-time basis. These therapists provided individuals or small groups various services, primarily in speech therapy, occupational therapy, physical therapy, Braille, mobility and orientation, adapted physical education, counseling, music therapy, and applied behavior analysis. Specialists working full or part-time taught classes in visual arts, movement, music, and science. A full-time nurse monitored and served students both in her office and throughout the building. The O'Hearn had one full-time administrator, one secretary, and one custodian. A part-time staff person facilitated IEP meetings and processed paperwork for students with special needs.

Because the O'Hearn was a magnet inclusion school with high concentration of students with moderate and significant disabilities, the co-teaching model with some part-time para-professional support was calculated to be cost-effective. If they had not attended the O'Hearn, some of our students would have attended separate public or private schools that served children with complex issues and were very expensive. Depending on the severity of the disability, many students would have been assigned to substantially separate classrooms within the district. These classrooms were usually staffed by one teacher and two or three paraprofessionals and served a total of just six or seven students. Many others would have attended substantially separate classes with one teacher and at least one paraprofessional serving between eight and twelve students. In addition to the high staffing costs of these specialized schools and separate classrooms, without the O'Hearn, some of our students would have been transported long distances at great expense to schools out of the East Zone of Boston. Whether or not children with significant disabilities were included, it cost a lot of money to educate them. When Boston utilized a weighted student formula that factored in the severity of students' needs, the cost-effectiveness of the O'Hearn was confirmed. In order to offer an excellent inclusive and high-quality learning experience for all, our budgetary rationale at the O'Hearn was to combine the same resources that would have been expended on our special-needs students in more restrictive settings along with our allocations for general-education students.

When inclusive education began at the O'Hearn in 1989, the term *integration* was used much more than the words *inclusion* or *inclusive education*. Boston had already been involved in a major court order mandating the integration of schools by race, and some schools had also been promoting the integration of students from different language groups. Although some students with disabilities had been included in Boston before 1989 in schools throughout the district, the O'Hearn was the first school in the system that was mandated to integrate students with a range of disabilities, including children with significant challenges, and to do so in all grades and in all classes.

Inclusive education was phased in over several years at the O'Hearn. In 1989, the program started in our early childhood and kindergarten classes. In 1990, it expanded into grades—one through three. A year later, we added grade four, and in 1992, we reached grade five. Thus, inclusion was initiated gradually over four years. From the perspective of our students who started inclusive education at a young age, integrating children with and without disabilities was the norm and to be expected, because they hadn't experienced any other arrangement.

The academic performance of students at the O'Hearn improved significantly with the introduction of inclusive education. Before students with disabilities were integrated, the overall (median) scores of O'Hearn students on standardized tests were below the national average. As the inclusion was phased in through grade five, scores rose and continued to improve. Under No Child Left Behind (NCLB) regulations, the school demonstrated that most students were able to achieve rigorous standards or make substantial progress toward them. According to the Massachusetts Comprehensive Assessment System (MCAS), O'Hearn students as a group usually scored at the high performing levels on both English/language arts and mathematics assessments, and children taking alternate assessments because of cognitive delays usually received high marks on their portfolios. Equally important, the samples of student work collected in assessment folders and the work displayed throughout the school on bulletin boards also demonstrated high quality, rigor, and creativity.

In addition to the school's overall strong academic standing, the O'Hearn rated high on other key indicators. In light of the number of requests made by parents using the Controlled Choice Student Assignment Plan, the O'Hearn was one of Boston's more popular schools. Student behavior and interactions within the school were generally positive. Staff turnover was relatively infrequent, and there were many applicants for any available openings on staff. The school hosted many visitors and received ample coverage in local and national media. Students' exhibitions and performances in the arts were highly regarded and well attended. Technology was widely used throughout the building. Much attention was focused on the school's high level of family involvement as well as its inclusion. Like all schools, there continued to be many areas for improvements, but inclusive education did not prove to be a detriment to teaching and learning. On the contrary, inclusion helped mobilize the school community to develop a more successful school for everyone.

During each of the twenty years that I served as principal, there were indeed some students who did not achieve as much as the staff or families desired. The O'Hearn, like schools everywhere, always had growth areas particularly in terms of helping individual students improve as much as they could academically, socially, and emotionally. A few families did elect to transfer their children out of the O'Hearn using Boston's Controlled Choice Student Assignment Plan, but this occurred at one of the lowest rates in the city. In addition, for some children with disabilities, the families and teachers decided, through the IEP process, that inclusive placement was not appropriate for this child, and thus they requested a substantially separate or private placement with smaller classes or different support. These cases were also quite rare and usually involved just 1 or 2 percent of the O'Hearn's total special education population.

All schools grapple with common priorities such as rigorous curriculum, effective instruction, meaningful professional development, positive school climate, informative assessments, and strong family involvement—all of which are key components in the quest for excellence. Because the O'Hearn was also committed to integrating so many students with disabilities, the entire school community had to focus on additional factors. We had to promote a culture of inclusion in which every student was validated for strengths, welcomed enthusiastically, and encouraged to achieve at high levels. We had to promote specialized and universally designed instruction, which allows students to access information, engage in activities, and show understanding at different levels in multiple ways. We also had to promote a higher level of collaboration, where everyone dedicated time and energy to planning and figuring out the best ways to help individual students learn and succeed. Focusing on these factors that were essential for students with disabilities created more enriched learning opportunities for students without disabilities—including children considered talented and gifted.

Building an effective inclusive school transformed teaching and learning at the O'Hearn. As principal, I was fortunate to collaborate with many terrific staff, families, students, and outside supporters who contributed greatly to this effort. The work was challenging but rewarding. The determination to help every child learn and succeed at high levels in inclusive classrooms was our critical first step.

Note: The Patrick O'Hearn Elementary School was renamed the Dr. William W. Henderson Inclusion School in June 2009 upon my retirement from the Boston Public Schools.

2

⬥

DETERMINATION: INCLUSION WILL WORK

THE STUDENT'S CHALLENGE

*"They told us that Franklin needed to go to a special school
and that he couldn't learn in a 'regular' class."*

These comments, made in my office by two discouraged parents, summarized what a neurologist and a school psychologist recommended regarding their three-year-old son, Franklin, who was diagnosed with autism. The parents recognized that he was not communicating at the typical developmental level, that he preferred to play by himself, and that he didn't like loud noises or changes in routines. But they also described him as energetic, insightful, and creative, and they could not fathom why others thought that he was not "good enough" to be included in our school.

Unfortunately, I have listened to many similar rejection stories from parents at the O'Hearn and from others around the country. These families had been told by medical or educational professionals that their sons or daughters should not be included in a typical class with their nondisabled peers. Such pronouncements have been made despite the fact that for decades, federal special education legislation has stipulated that the regular-education classroom, with appropriate support, should be the first consideration for students. These laws have not negated the continuum of more restrictive settings, including substantially separate classrooms and private placements. As described in chapter 1, some O'Hearn students did not make all the progress that staff and parents would have liked, and occasionally, during a review of a student's IEP (Individualized Education Program), another placement was recommended. Overall, these cases were very rare and usually occurred because the IEP team believed that the child needed to try a smaller setting to make more progress.

I found, however, that the vast majority of parents, like Franklin's mother and father, who received recommendations from professionals to place their children in substantially separate classes or schools, were advised to do so without the professionals' even first considering general-education classrooms with appropriate support and services. After listening to such stories from parents, I would usually point out that even some experts do not recognize all that is possible for children with disabilities, and I would briefly share my own encounter with misguided recommendations from my doctor and educational leader. Parents expressed surprised hearing about my experiences, and some agreed that the professionals that they encountered didn't always understand everything that their child could do. I would then suggest to the parents that no expert could predict for sure how a child with a disability would perform in a general-education classroom, but that if they never tried it, they might never know. Thus I encouraged parents to consider inclusion first, as long as there were educators willing to welcome their child, provide the necessary support, and work hard to ensure success.

Because Franklin's parents were determined that he should be included, the Special Education Department of the Boston Public Schools agreed to assign him to the O'Hearn. Over the years, Franklin showed us that he was a strong learner. In addition to the general curricula, he received services twice a week from a speech therapist, who helped him with communication, and once a week from an occupational therapist, who focused on sensory integration and fine motor skills. His special education and regular-education teachers supported him by offering specific strategies for social interaction and for transitions from one activity to another. Through hard work and excellent teaching, his literacy and mathematics skills eventually developed to well above grade level, and he learned how to complete most assignments quite independently.

Franklin did demonstrate some of the social awkwardness typical of many students on the autism spectrum. When his friends were joking around, he sometimes took things too seriously, so staff gave him suggestions for more playful and appropriate responses. When his teachers made a mistake while solving a complex math problem, he sometimes corrected them, sounding too much like a know-it-all, so we taught him some ways that he could be more discreet. Over the years, he learned to interact more comfortably with others. His classmates certainly recognized his intellect, and they regularly asked him to share his insights and suggestions. Franklin eventually overcame his reluctance to perform in the O'Hearn's many plays and classroom exhibitions, and he was usually quite impressive in these endeavors.

At the end of every school year in Boston, Mayor Thomas Menino invited two students from each of the city's public schools to attend an award ceremony at the historic Faneuil Hall. In June of his fifth grade, Franklin was the O'Hearn student who was selected to represent the school for top academic honors. He earned the award on the basis of his class work and test scores. His family and the whole O'Hearn community were very proud of him. Franklin's mother made sure to send a picture of him holding his trophy and standing between the mayor and the superintendent to the neurologist who had advised that he not be included at our school.

Upon leaving the O'Hearn, Franklin attended an advanced work class at a nearby middle school for grade six. He continued to achieve at high levels there, and in light of his grades and scores on standardized tests, he was accepted by a Boston high school that served advanced students in grades seven through twelve. Except for monthly check-ins with an occupational therapist, he did not receive any other special education services, but a sensitive guidance counselor kept close tabs on him. Franklin graduated from high school with honors and went on to college to major in engineering. His mother adamantly maintained that her determination to include him at a young age not only helped to maximize his academic progress but also improved his social development, and she was convinced that his inclusion allowed him to be much better prepared for college than if he had stayed in a small and separate classroom.

THE PRINCIPAL'S CHALLENGE

Most principals need and benefit from a little extra drive. Disabilities helped me develop more feistiness, first from dealing with my own eye condition and then from trying to include many students with significant challenges. I will never forget when I was twelve and my father confronted me with the news that I probably would not realize my childhood dream of becoming a professional football player, because of my recent diagnosis with RP. His discouraging words incited me to play even harder and to organize my own team. I played quarterback and linebacker. Throwing passes downfield and tackling opponents felt great, but that was just a short reprieve. My doctor would not sign the permission form for me to play high school football, even though I was a good athlete and my daytime vision was almost normal. That was devastating for me, and I was too ashamed to tell anyone. I did join the high school's cross-country and tennis teams, though, and, in my senior year, became <u>captain</u> of <u>both</u>.

In college, I told very few people that I had RP and could not see well in the dark. I was embarrassed about this and could hide it most of the time, thanks to the well-lit city streets. In 1970, after my second year at Yale, I set off solo for Peru, where I was forced to deal with my vision impairment openly for the first time. I volunteered to work in a mountainous and rural area of the Andes, where thousands of people had been killed and where most houses had been demolished by a major earthquake. I helped carry and distribute relief goods (food, blankets, clothing, and some medicine) to many small villages that were located as high as eleven thousand feet above sea level. We carried these items on donkeys and on our backs, making our way slowly along precipitous cliffs and around much rubble. I also helped clear debris and build adobe houses. There was no electricity in most of the villages, so at nighttime, we only had the light from the moon and stars, and I had no other options but to tell folks around me that I could not see in the dark. The Peruvians treated this as if it were no big deal. I just held on to someone's elbow or shoulder when moving around at night, but I still carried my load and, often, some of the items of the person who was guiding me. This experience traversing mountains in the dark provided me with the first hint that I could still be active and contribute even without sight.

Being told by an eye doctor and subsequently by a school administrator to get out of education while I was a young and fairly productive teacher was indeed demoralizing, but it helped me become more determined. I resented their insinuations that I could not continue to succeed as an educator, being blind. I knew I needed support from others, starting with family and friends. Connecting with blind persons associated with local and national organizations provided critical modeling and guidance. In addition to advocating for rights and opportunities, the National Federation of the Blind (NFB) and other organizations offered many examples of how blind individuals could be respectable and contribute. Accepting my blindness and developing new skills were key. I definitely became more tenacious. Neither my blindness nor others' negative perception about it was going to keep me from being an effective educator.

One of my first responsibilities as principal at the O'Hearn was to build a team that was determined to succeed. Developing effective inclusive schools requires strong resolve. When we started including students with disabilities in 1989, many critics told us that it was a bad idea, particularly when we involved students with significant impairments. Basically, the naysayers believed that neither the students with disabilities nor the students without disabilities would learn as much as they would if instructed in separate classrooms. All of the staff who had been working at the O'Hearn before inclusion started were given the option of transferring to another Boston school. Most decided to stay and committed to trying their best. A few did opt to leave. One person who transferred out admitted that he was doing so because "the handicapped" were coming. To be successful, we needed staff who felt excited about working both with children who had disabilities and with children without disabilities. We also needed staff who would dedicate the extra effort to learn how to promote inclusion while still fulfilling their regular teaching responsibilities.

Before the students arrived in September 1989, I spoke individually with each teacher assigned to the O'Hearn about general concerns and other ideas. In relation to inclusion, most expressed a willingness to stay and try to make it work. I respected the honesty of one teacher who said that she wanted to see how it developed in the kindergarten classes before committing for the following years. She did choose to remain and proved to be excellent. A veteran teacher shared that he had always thought it unfair that the kids with cognitive delays in his neighborhood never had a chance to attend the same schools with their friends. Another teacher who had worked at the O'Hearn before inclusion remarked how pleased she felt that the students with special needs would no longer be separated. Some of the new and existing teachers talked passionately about their own family members with disabilities—people whom they tried to involve in their homes and communities. Other new teachers indicated that they had been troubled about always having to teach the kids with disabilities in their other schools in such isolated settings. A few teachers even shared with me how they were managing their own chronic problems, some of which were known by others but some of which were private.

Overall, that first year, a dedicated team of teachers seemed determined to make inclusive education work. Inclusion got off to a fairly good start in the kindergarten classrooms, and the interactions among the young children were quite positive. Early on during that first year, however, I encountered a challenge, and it occurred in a place where the culture of a school always seems to make itself evident: the school cafeteria.

For lunch periods, O'Hearn teachers typically escorted their classes to the cafeteria and left students with lunch monitors or paraprofessionals who supervised the children while the teachers ate their lunches either in the small teachers' room or in their classrooms. Although the lunch staff and paraprofessionals were aware that the school was including students with disabilities, these adults had not been involved with any of the training that had occurred before the opening of school. The kindergarten teachers stayed in the cafeteria to help assist their young students for the first week, but, by the second week, took a well-deserved break and left their students with the lunch staff.

Although some of the disabilities of O'Hearn students were clearly visible, others were not. Unfortunately, one lunch monitor brusquely ordered a boy who had autism and who physically appeared typical to get up, throw away his scraps in the barrel, and then line up for recess. In his previous school, the boy had always stayed in a basement room for all his classes and for lunch with just five other kids and up to four adults.

Someone always had cleaned up for him or had held his hand when it was time to get in line. For his first independent attempt in the O'Hearn cafeteria, the boy managed to get half of his leftovers into the barrel, but the other portion spilled onto the floor, which was still shining brightly from its summer stripping and waxing. The boy who made the mess was mostly nonverbal, and he started jumping near the barrel and making a chuckling noise. One of the lunch monitors on duty blurted out the word "idiot." Since the boy sometimes echoed emotional words that he heard, he responded by repeatedly shouting "idiot" back at her.

The adult who called the boy an idiot clearly acted inappropriately, and I dealt directly with her, following Boston Public School procedures. She was not aware that the boy had a disability, and she acknowledged that the word "idiot" should not be used anytime in our school. After talking with her, I recognized that in addition to the professional development that was ongoing for teachers, we needed to dedicate some time preparing all the support staff for inclusion. The lunch staff and paraprofessionals met with me, and we set some ground rules. The teachers helped by providing explicit strategies that the support staff were expected to use. I hoped that things were getting better.

The next week, still in my first month as principal, the president of the union representing Boston's lunch workers appeared at my office. She asserted that her members should not have to "serve the handicapped." I was flabbergasted and felt offended and irate. After calming myself, I stated unequivocally that the O'Hearn was now an inclusive school and that everyone who worked here would be supporting all kids, including those with disabilities. From a historical perspective, the union president was partly correct. Lunch staff had seldom "served the handi-capped," because those students were usually kept apart and taken care of by their own teachers or special paraprofessionals. With inclusion, students with disabilities would now be partici-pating in classes and activities throughout the building, and all staff members would have to be prepared for varying levels of support. We definitely needed to provide training for the lunch staff at the O'Hearn, but the willingness to serve students with and without disabilities in inclusive settings was nonnegotia-ble. With input from teachers and parents, a number of changes were instituted to improve the climate and procedures in the cafeteria. By the end of that first year, of all the four staff who had previously worked many years with O'Hearn students dur-ing lunch, one tragically died of a heart attack, one retired, one transferred to another school, and the one who had called the boy an "idiot" stayed and proved quite helpful.

All principals strive to develop a staff that is dedicated to the mission of their schools. This leadership challenge was crystal-lized early on for me. It was ultimately my responsibility to en-sure that all O'Hearn staff were committed to, as well as skill-ful in, making inclusion work. I recognized that we would have to learn much along the way, but I also communicated clearly that the staff's determination to help children with and without disabilities learn and succeed together was not just essential—it was expected.

IMPLICATIONS FOR THE SCHOOL

Over the years, the staff and I heard many other stories express-ing doubts about the ability of individual students to achieve at the O'Hearn. Many parents besides Franklin's shared how a medical or educational professional had discouraged them from enrolling their child in inclusive classrooms because of the child's "special needs." Some parents related how some "experts" had recommended that their child with a disability be removed from our school even after the student had made much progress with us. In addition, the O'Hearn received many students who had transferred from, or had been counseled out of, parochial, charter, or other district schools because of issues that others felt could not be adequately addressed. Dealing with so many children who had or who were expected to experience major learning problems was extra challenging. Excellent teaching would be essential, but the determination to help every child learn and succeed in an inclusive environment was the critical first step.

After my first year, all staff who worked at the O'Hearn were well aware that inclusive education was mandated as well as central to our mission. Levels of commitment, though, are manifested more in daily words and actions than in general statements. O'Hearn staff members needed to regularly demonstrate their high expectations for all students to learn and succeed in inclusive classrooms. To foster a positive culture of inclusion, we needed to promote disability awareness, highlighting the potential and accomplishments of persons with disabilities. We also needed to develop a stronger community in which individuals would show leadership and speak up on behalf of inclusion whenever it was warranted.

Throughout the twenty years that I was principal, many members of the O'Hearn community responded directly and eloquently to cynicism expressed by outsiders about inclusion. Usually, community members did this by sharing their successful experiences and other relevant data. It was most impressive for me, though, to witness how many spoke up within the school in ways that showed strong conviction and even some courage. For example:

- When staff members focused too much on students' impairments, others pointed out the need to build on children's strengths and shared recommendations to promote success.
- When parents questioned whether their children would learn next to students with intellectual disabilities, other parents described the advantages that the experience provided.
- When support staff maintained that no one wanted to play with particular children who had significant challenges at recess, the teachers and students responded by figuring out ways to facilitate meaningful participation.
- When therapists pulled out students too frequently for interventions, teachers suggested ways to appropriately offer more services in classrooms.
- When bus monitors asserted that it was impossible for "those special kids" to ride on their buses, teachers and parents offered tips and procedures for a safe and pleasant ride.
- When teachers complained too much about having to teach skills in a class with so many diverse needs, others acknowledged the challenges but highlighted effective strategies.
- When staff members neglected to provide accommodations on a regular basis for students with specific learning disabilities, others articulated the critical importance of particular programs offering text and speech.

Occasionally, I needed to work with particular staff regarding the situations listed above or regarding other concerns about their commitment to helping all children learn and succeed in inclusive settings. In the vast majority of cases, direct conversations, along with ongoing professional development, were sufficient. The Boston evaluation instruments were sometimes useful. Employee disciplinary procedures were utilized on rare occasions. Helping children learn and succeed in inclusive classrooms at high levels was clearly not negotiable, though, and we were determined to make it work.

Interestingly, it was the experience of inclusion that most helped changed people's thinking about it. Having so many students with disabilities in general-education classrooms expanded the students' and staff's perspectives on the will to achieve. On a regular basis, many students extended tremendous efforts to complete a variety of tasks that most others consider basic. Some of these regular experiences that made impressions on others included the following:

- A third-grade boy with Down syndrome trying hard to point to and sound out the words in his adapted books
- A fifth-grade girl with cerebral palsy focusing her energy to manipulate an adapted keyboard connected to a computer in order to write an eloquent and persuasive essay
- A fourth-grade student with speech impairments proudly presenting to the class his report on a state using assistive technology
- A second-grade student with fingers malformed on both hands maneuvering objects to solve math problems
- A fifth-grade boy propelling his wheelchair with his arms to keep up with his running classmates at recess

- A kindergarten student with intellectual disabilities attempting to emulate her classmates who were reading, even though she held her book upside down
- A fifth-grade girl with autism and significant communication disorders standing in front of others and reciting a poem

The students' determination to succeed at tasks that most others would consider basic presented a different perspective on achievement. How could we really know what students with significant disabilities (or we) could accomplish if we did not try? Abilities are developed starting with effort and resolve. In an inclusive school like the O'Hearn, it was not so easy to make excuses for not trying hard to do one's best. The determination and efforts of children with the most significant disabilities helped motivate the staff and all the students to perform at higher levels.

This did not mean that all students who had disabilities always worked hard and up to their potential. Staff and parents frequently had to intervene so that their children would try harder and do more. Some students with disabilities even occasionally tried to use their impairments as an excuse. Lowered expectations because of disabilities—whether these expectations are expressed by others or internalized by the students themselves—are not acceptable. We were steadfast in our convictions that students with disabilities would learn and succeed. Thus we challenged both our students with intellectual disabilities and those who were advanced to read or be read to as much as possible. We challenged our students with speech disorders and our most eloquent speakers to communicate as effectively as possible. And we challenged both our students with mobility impairments and our fastest runners to exercise as much as possible. Pushing students with disabilities to do their best was critical for them, and it set a tone for the other students in our school.

At the O'Hearn, the performance of students without disabilities was also critical. Before we introduced inclusive education, overall academic achievement had been at the below-average level. Many parents had typically pulled their children out of the school after kindergarten and had enrolled them in a nearby parochial school. Other parents had kept their children in the school through grade three, hoping to have them invited to one of Boston's advanced-work classes, which started at grade four in other designated schools. Because of these practices, there used to be many vacancies at the O'Hearn. To be a successful inclusive school for all children, we needed to reverse those trends. Parents of general-education students expressed that they would be happy to keep their children in an inclusive environment, but wanted their children to experience a more academically rigorous and engaging curricula that would help them learn and succeed at high levels. We believed and were determined to demonstrate that O'Hearn students without disabilities could achieve at least as well as, if not better than, they could in another school without inclusion.

Over the years, the overall performance of both students with disabilities and those without did improve, and the O'Hearn gained a reputation as a high-achieving school. Most of the parents whose children qualified for advanced-work programs elected to keep them at the O'Hearn. They recognized, and officials from the School Department confirmed, that our students considered to be talented and gifted (some of whom had a disability) were indeed participating in stimulating and challenging curricula. Inclusion proved to be a great experience for almost everyone at the O'Hearn. In fact, as will be described in upcoming chapters, we came to recognize how implementing inclusive education helped us enhance all students' performance. The determination to make inclusion work for everyone was our critical first step.

3

✼

VISION: A MULTI-ABLED LEARNING COMMUNITY WITH MANY PATHS TOWARD SUCCESS

THE STUDENT'S CHALLENGE

*"I want Maria to be learning and having fun
with the other kids."*

This is the vision for Maria that her parents shared with teachers and therapists the week before she was assigned to our grade one class. Maria had multiple disabilities with profound cognitive delays. She could not walk, talk, or feed herself, and her vision and hearing were also impaired. Maria was developmentally at a level typical of a one-year-old. Her parents kept emphasizing that she was "a good girl" who loved being around "regular kids" like her cousins. Maria had been attending a substantially separate class in another school farther away and out of zone with five other children with significant impairments (none of the children could talk). The class was taught by one teacher and two paraprofessionals. The parents had requested a transfer and were ecstatic to hear that she would be transferred to the O'Hearn, where she would be learning with nondisabled peers in the same school that two of her cousins attended. Her new class would have fifteen students without disabilities, four students with mild to moderate disabilities, and three other students with complex issues. The class would be taught by two teachers and one paraprofessional and would receive support from therapists as stipulated in the students' IEPs.

One of Maria's new classmates was George, a young boy who had cerebral palsy. He used a wheelchair, and it took him a little longer to speak and to manipulate objects. George was an avid reader, and he loved to write stories. He acted shyly sometimes in large groups, but interacted comfortably in small groups and played with classmates in the courtyard. George's parents had expressed aspirations for him similar to the vision voiced by Maria's parents. They wanted him to learn as much as possible and have fun with the other kids.

Although Maria and George both used wheelchairs and had obvious disabilities, they were quite different academically. Maria was functioning at an extremely low level, while George, according to assessments used in the district, was performing near the top of his group. Despite these academic disparities, they were members of the same class. Their teachers would strive to help both of them as well as their other classmates with varying abilities to learn and succeed. This would require a great deal of flexibility and creativity, but the vision for their class, as well as the others in the school, would be the same. Their class should be a vibrant learning community that would utilize multiple strategies for teaching and learning to help all children achieve at the highest possible levels.

Like most of the students in the class, George would be expected to meet or exceed the same standards throughout the curricula that were designated for grade one students in Boston. He would have access to an adapted keyboard and to pencils and crayons with special grips to assist with writing and drawing. Each week, he would receive a few hours of additional support from speech and occupational therapists in the classroom and from a physical therapist during movement class and recess. He would get assistance from a paraprofessional or a teacher with toileting. Most of the time, though, he was working individually or with his classmates on tasks at levels stipulated by standards in the general curricula.

Maria would need alternate standards and much additional support. The staff examined her previous IEP and concurred that a major focus would continue to be on sensory stimulation and basic communication. The major difference was that her instruction and therapies would now occur primarily in a general-education classroom with many other children. Maria used a computer and headphones to see and listen to books. A touch screen and large switch were utilized to help her make choices. She would manipulate large objects. More than anything, though, her smiles and vocalizations communicated how she really enjoyed being around the other children. Although Maria took more breaks and visited the sensory integration room for a short time each afternoon, she spent most of the day sitting among her classmates during the regularly scheduled whole class and small group lessons. She followed along and generally enjoyed participating in activities throughout the school, including lunch and recess. Often, another adult (teacher, therapist, or paraprofessional) would be directly assisting her, but many times, the other children would just naturally involve her while going about their business, simply by asking her if she liked the story that the teacher read or by guiding her hand with the big crayon on the picture that they were making.

Maria's multiple disabilities and extreme cognitive delays did not go away. As evidenced by her happy smiles and vocalizations, Maria certainly enjoyed coming to the O'Hearn and being with her friends. She learned to communicate more by increasing her repertoire of gestures, utterances, and manipulations of simple devices. She participated eagerly in most class activities and school-wide events, albeit with much assistance, particularly in helping her move around and eat. Maria's family was most grateful for the natural and wonderful support provided by her classmates and recognized how important it was for her cousins who attended the O'Hearn to see Maria mingling so well with other kids. It helped the cousins feel more comfortable and even proud about being with her in public.

After the O'Hearn, Maria attended a collaborative program outside the district for middle school and high school. When she became a young adult, and after much advocacy by her parents, Maria moved into a small community residence that was designed for adults with disabilities and that always had staff support. She participated in a day program that offers some basic vocational and recreational experiences. Some of Maria's classmates from the O'Hearn continued to meet her in the Boston area. Her mother appreciated how eagerly these former classmates greeted and connected with her, and the mother acknowledged that Maria helped teach many of her peers about human diversity and compassion.

George, who developed into one of the top students at the O'Hearn, usually performed at advanced levels. He participated actively in classes, and his insights and other contributions were valued by staff and peers. George earned major roles in a number of the school's plays. He was also a popular student who made many friends.

For his middle and high school years, George attended a local charter school, which did a good job accommodating him. However, students who had intellectual disabilities were not encouraged to attend that same school and did not fare as well there. George continued to be an excellent student, and he participated on the debating team and drama club. In the summers, George attended an inclusive camp for students with and without disabilities; he eventually became a counselor at the summer camp. Upon graduation from high school, he enrolled in one of the state universities, where he majored in history, participated in clubs and other activities, and acted as an advocate for disability issues. Although he still received support from part-time personal care attendants for activities of daily living, including dressing and bathing, he managed quite independently otherwise and navigated comfortably around the campus in his wheelchair.

THE PRINCIPAL'S CHALLENGE

Because I became blind, I needed to learn how to complete some work and perform some responsibilities in other ways. Like many students with disabilities at the O'Hearn, I needed to learn how to read, write, and compute using different strategies. When I started as principal in 1989, I could still see a little and utilized equipment that allowed me to magnify and darken the print from written documents onto a monitor. That technology was relatively easy to use since all I had to do was turn a few knobs adjusting the size and intensity of the letters and slide the tray under the monitor so that I could move the printed page to the place where I wanted to read. Reading was more laborious for me with this equipment, though, and soon thereafter, my vision decreased to a point that it was no longer efficient.

Although I had started studying Braille before becoming principal, I still needed to learn a lot more about deciphering its many codes and using different tools to write it. A young man from the Massachusetts Commission for the Blind came to the O'Hearn after the regular school day and gave me some lessons in Braille. Interestingly, some of our students who participated in the after-school program asked him which school he was in charge of, assuming that anyone with a white cane must be a principal. With his support and a lot of practice, I learned Braille well enough to use it regularly for reading short documents, writing notes, and making labels.

I also learned how to use some new software that allowed me to hear text and navigate while writing Word documents and using e-mail or the Internet. A technology specialist from the Commission for the Blind (who was also blind himself) came out to the school and taught me how to use the software. He also demonstrated the program to a technology specialist from the Boston Public Schools so that I could get ongoing support with any problems and anticipated upgrades. Although I learned how to write memos and reports and how to deal with the many e-mails fairly independently, accessing Web sites both within and outside the Boston School Department was much trickier. Over the years, accessibility did improve, but there have always been some sites and specific programs that were more difficult for me to use.

Computing was easy for me to do being blind. I had a good sense of numbers and could solve a lot of math mentally. Talking calculators took care of the more involved problems. The only problem was that sometimes, folks liked to borrow my talking calculator and didn't always return it to the right place. When it came to the school's finances, I relied on the help of the school's secretary for check writing and payroll completion. The people in the budget office of the Boston School Department were also gracious in helping me fill out any required forms. I kept the limited cash that we received from bake sales or raffles in a locked cabinet and separated the bills in different envelopes. This worked fine most of the time, but once I did tip a pizza delivery woman with a very unusual hundred-dollar bill instead of a five-dollar bill. Fortunately, she knew one of our parents and was very honest.

Being blind, I also needed to figure out how to do physical exercise differently. As exercise was critical for my emotional well-being, I had always engaged in some physical activity almost every day. When I first became a principal, I was still able to see enough to run alone on an empty track early in the morning. Soon thereafter, my running was on a treadmill, or with a guide. Bicycling took place on a tandem or on a stationary bike. Kayaking had to happen with a companion. I kept up with gardening and utilized twine and stakes to follow the plants and keep me oriented. At the local Dorchester Y, I was able to swim by having ropes on each side of the lane and counting my strokes. I also enjoyed using the universal weight machines in the gym and either felt and counted the holes to move the pins or turn the knobs to select my desired amount of resistance. Navigating with my white cane from one weight machine to another was easy enough unless someone was resting on a piece of equipment and I didn't hear them. People learned to speak up to avoid having me on their laps.

I really missed not being able to drive. Fortunately, we lived near public transportation, which I used fairly regularly. I also hitched a lot of rides from family, staff, and friends. On the positive side, my blindness meant that I saved some money not needing a second car and that the School Department did not need to reimburse me for parking or mileage expenses that were sometimes available for principals.

As I continued to lose my sight, I kept doing almost everything that I needed or wanted to do, but I did have to learn how to do some things differently. Some of the changes, such as using Braille, involved study and practice, while others, like using plastic dots to identify the thirty-second marker of the microwave oven, were quite easy. My experiences with my own personal adjustments undoubtedly helped prepare me to lead a school that needed to provide lots of adaptations. Accommodations and modifications were essential for many students to participate meaningfully in the life of the school and to advance academically. All principals need to recognize that there are many paths toward success, and we need to identify the right ones and teach children how to access them. Blindness forced me not only to utilize but also to appreciate the multiple ways of learning. Unfortunately, some educators still think that one standard method is sufficient or the best approach for everyone. I now believe that denying students appropriate tools and strategies to help them learn in different and often more efficient ways is a form of educational malpractice.

IMPLICATIONS FOR THE SCHOOL

When we first started inclusion at the O'Hearn in 1989, we were not entirely sure how we were going to do it, particularly

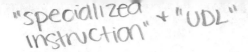
"specialized instruction" + "UDL"

with the students like Maria, who had more significant intellectual disabilities. Our vision was to help all students learn and succeed, but given the diversity of needs, we knew that we had to allow for many different paths for learning. Right from the beginning, we identified the arts and technology as key components of our curricula at the O'Hearn. Specialized instruction remained essential, and universal design for learning (UDL, described later in the chapter) emerged soon thereafter as another critical strategy.

Arts

In September 1989, the first month of inclusion at the O'Hearn, a deputy superintendent who supervised me and the school provided us with a $5,000 grant. He suggested that we connect with an organization called Very Special Arts of Massachusetts (now referred to as VSA Massachusetts). That initial funding served as a catalyst for a long-term relationship that helped transform teaching and learning at our school. With those funds, we were able to contract with visiting teaching artists who had experience involving students with disabilities in arts activities. Usually, these artists worked with four or five classes over a few months for a total of about ten to fifteen sessions per class.

During the first couple of years of inclusion, talented teaching artists from VSA Massachusetts contributed to the O'Hearn in many creative ways, including these:

- A visual artist helped our students design beautiful murals for our walls and the facade of the building. These murals, which celebrated both the diversity of our students and the commonality of our mission, came with accompanying slogans such as "We Are All Special" and

51

"Learning Together and From Each Other." Through this project, the artist also helped us figure out how to include students who couldn't see the paintings and students who couldn't hold paintbrushes in their hands.

- A musician helped our students sing and create songs that highlighted the importance of community and reinforced vocabulary development. He also helped us figure out how to include students who could not speak or understand the meaning of many of the lyrics in the songs they were singing.

- A dance specialist helped our students learn innovative routines and demonstrate the movements of animals and the human skeletal system. She also helped us figure out how to include students who could not walk and students who had difficulties following directions.

- A drama teacher helped students depict historical situations and the personalities of characters from literature. She found ways to include students who could not read the printed script and students who were uncomfortable performing in front of others.

- An amazing discovery from these arts internships was that not only were students with significant issues participating and learning more with their nondisabled peers, but all the students were benefiting tremendously from the creative and flexible approaches necessary for these multi-abled arts experiences. The arts clearly embellished the curriculum and engaged students in meaningful activities. Parents and teachers who were representatives on the O'Hearn School Site Council, the decision-making organization for the school, advocated even more arts experiences. Utilizing the school's budget allocation for specialists, the council recommended hiring two full-time arts teachers who had experience with inclusion. The council also decided to commit to a long-term partner-ship with VSA Massachusetts.

Over the years, the O'Hearn's arts teachers and the teaching artists from VSA Massachusetts and from other Boston cultural agencies were instrumental in designing and implementing quality arts experiences in visual arts, music, movement, and drama during both the regular school day and the after-school program. In addition to the many dynamic classroom experiences, the arts team helped coordinate annual school-wide performances. These included a show done that focused on children's literature and was performed by the younger students, a drama centered on important events in African American history, a depiction of a well-known play or musical by older students, a talent show, and other recitals and cultural presentations. The quality of these performances was highly regarded, and usually over 250 parents and community supporters packed the school auditorium. I believe that most parents of children with and without disabilities yearn to be involved in their children's education, particularly when the adults can witness the children's learning and progress. The arts have been instrumental in boosting family involvement at the O'Hearn.

The arts team and visiting artists also collaborated extensively with classroom teachers to figure out ways to better integrate the arts throughout the entire curriculum. The arts proved to be an excellent tool to help students learn important concepts, vocabulary, and facts in subjects like English language arts, social studies, science, and even mathematics. The infusion of the arts throughout the various curricula motivated and engaged students in activities that introduced and reinforced many skills and much knowledge. Teachers and parents recognized how the arts were instrumental in enhancing overall student achievement, and they have committed to keeping the arts a top school priority.

Technology

Because of their disabilities, many O'Hearn students had major difficulties learning traditionally. Technology offers tools that allow students to access curricula and to engage in lessons and activities in different ways. Staff from the Boston Public Schools offices of technology and special education services collaborated with us and provided some materials and much training. We also connected with organizations like the Center for Applied Special Technology (CAST), Kurzweil (an assistive-technology company), Easter Seals, and Intel to recommend additional hardware and software. We hustled continuously to acquire what our students needed.

Over the years, O'Hearn students utilized many devices and programs daily to accommodate their unique and specific needs. For example, for reading, many students utilized cassettes, talking digital players, software offering text and speech, books with tactile objects and recorded sounds, computerized books with pictures and voice, or devices with Braille and speech. For writing, students could use minicomputers, laptops, adapted keyboards, special switches, special grips, speech-to-text programs, or tools for writing Braille. For computation, there were traditional calculators, adapted calculators, and various interactive computer programs. And for speech, students used equipment with prerecorded responses, programs with pictures and symbols reflecting choice and responses, or devices that converted keyboard input into voice.

Many of these programs and devices were offered at no cost by regional libraries and by nonprofit organizations that support individuals with disabilities. Some technologies were provided by the Boston School Department, and a few others were paid for by private medical insurance. Still others were either donated or purchased through extensive fund-raising efforts. For most O'Hearn students with disabilities, the use of some technology was the only way that they could access the curricula. Other students with milder disabilities also benefited because the technology allowed them to complete more work at higher levels. Using technology, many more O'Hearn students with disabilities achieved at proficient or advanced levels on the rigorous district and state standards, and students with cognitive delays were able to make better progress toward their alternate goals.

It was, of course, exciting to witness the progress that many students with disabilities made using the varying technologies. It was also interesting to see how many students without disabilities were motivated to work harder and longer if they, too, could also try out some of the new equipment and software. Staff wisely provided increasing opportunities for students without disabilities to use more of the technology, even though some of the programs had originally been designed for children with disabilities. The parent and teacher leaders recognized the potential of technology for all students. The O'Hearn School Site Council made the increased use of technology as a regular tool for learning a priority, and plans for expanding technology throughout the school were developed.

In addition to the specialized equipment tailored for individual students with specific needs, each classroom received at least four computers with Internet access. With support from Intel, the school acquired a set of laptop computers on a rolling cart that teachers took turns scheduling for an entire class. Representatives from Kurzweil helped us purchase software licenses at a reduced cost because the O'Hearn was one of the first schools in Boston to pilot the company's program. Kurzweil allowed students with print disabilities to both see and hear text, and it offered many sources of support to facilitate writing.

With some initial funds from technology innovation grants, the school also acquired and purchased licenses for Web-based programs that differentiated materials according to skill level. These programs allowed students to access the materials in school, in their homes, or at other sites, including public libraries. Achieve 3000, one company offering these Web-based programs, provided nonfiction articles or information text with accompanying higher-order comprehension questions. Another company, First in Math, offered activities in various domains of mathematics. Both of these Web-based programs were ideally suited for inclusive classrooms with students working at, above, or below grade levels. This allowed for differentiated instruction, as students in the same class studied the same content at very different skill levels. Both companies also helped teachers and principals monitor students' individual progress in school and at home with detailed, computerized reports.

Professional development was essential with all this new technology. Extensive training and technical assistance around the new programs and equipment were provided by the district and outside agencies. Many hours of the school's in-service and teacher meeting times were dedicated to technology, and a few consultants provided tremendous support. A number of O'Hearn staff developed strong expertise in the various new programs. Their leadership and collaboration were instrumental in helping other teachers build their capacity to implement technology more effectively with all their students.

Specialized Instruction

Teaching children with disabilities forced us to expand our repertoire of instructional strategies. Some students needed and received specialized interventions on a regular basis. For example:

- Some blind students read and wrote every day using Braille.
- Some students with autism learned basic language through applied behavioral analysis (ABA).
- Some students with specific learning disabilities practiced decoding and phonemic awareness through intensive reading intervention and multisensory programs.
- Some students with speech and language impairments utilized special techniques and devices for oral communication.
- Some students with intellectual disabilities benefited from a software program with accompanying pictures and symbols to be introduced to basic literacy.

The classmates of these students who received the specialized instruction were usually curious about these specialized tools and approaches, and teachers regularly explained their value and use. However, interventions like these were not usually needed or appropriate as daily instructional strategies for most of the general population.

Sometimes, specialized learning needed to take place apart from the other students and, sometimes, even out of the general classroom. This was, technically speaking, not purely inclusive. For example, as math became more abstract and complex, we found much of the regular curriculum was neither realistic nor meaningful, particularly for the older students with significant intellectual disabilities. Converting fractions to decimals and solving long-division problems did not make sense for those who were still learning how to count their cents. During math time, students with intellectual disabilities often moved to a separate area of their classroom to work on material that was quite different from that of their peers.

Occasionally, they left the classroom and walked or wheeled to another area of the school to practice more functional math skills. For example, at the O'Hearn Baking Cafe, students with intellectual disabilities cooked tasty treats and, in the process, practiced measuring, mixing, communicating, and eating techniques. At the O'Hearn School Store, students sold items and thereby practiced labeling, advertising, handling money, and making sales. Other students practiced organizing, counting, record keeping, and transport when they worked at the O'Hearn Main Supply Closet. There was also a sensory integration area for special exercises, a speech room, and a small meeting room for mental health counseling.

Thus, we were never purists about inclusion at the O'Hearn. Students with disabilities did not need to be with their nondisabled peers every minute of the day. Frankly, this was impossible, particularly for the few students who were on special toileting schedules. However, it was indeed important for us that students with disabilities felt part of the classroom community and that they participated in lessons and activities with their nondisabled peers for the vast majority of each day. We always tried to minimize the amount of time that students spent apart from their nondisabled peers and to maximize the ways that services could be integrated in class routines without interrupting the flow of teaching and learning. Most of the time, this worked well, but it was not always perfect.

Universal Design for Learning (UDL)

Many other approaches and programs at the O'Hearn were used regularly and proved beneficial to all students, even though these programs had initially been intended for students with particular disabilities. As described above, we unleashed the potential of the arts and technology for enhancing teaching and learning for all students only after we had utilized these methods to assist students with special needs. The integration of arts and technology throughout the O'Hearn promoted what is sometimes referred to as *universal design for learning* (UDL). This meant that we utilized the power of the arts and technology to provide multiple creative ways that would help all our students to access information, engage in class activities, and demonstrate understanding.

A wonderful example of how the arts and technology were integrated and exemplified UDL in action was the fifth-grade unit on Native Americans. As part of their social studies curriculum, fifth-grade students spent a few weeks studying the life of Native Americans in New England during the 1600s. A major component of the unit was that all students were expected to find information about a specific tribe, and they did this in different ways using a variety of sources:

- School textbook or other books at various levels from local libraries
- Grade- or ability-appropriate information from the Internet
- Digital books through programs that also converted the print into audio or to Braille dots
- Stories written and illustrated for children at a lower developmental level and acquired either in print or displayed through computers
- Lessons and materials that teachers in other districts had written and that were accessed through the Internet

In addition to reading and writing about their particular Native American group, all students participated in a variety of whole-class or small-group activities:

- All students adopted a Native American name and learned a few other words from their particular tribe.
- All students listened to and sang or signed the words of some Native American songs.
- Some students practiced particular dances.
- Some students designed and painted murals and pictures.
- Some students designed short role-play skits.
- All students were asked to work at home to create a diorama or some objects depicting a cultural aspect of the culture of the group that they were studying. The teachers sent home guidelines and resources for this home project.

Finally, all students were asked to demonstrate what they had learned. This, too, happened in different ways. For example, most students, except those who had intellectual disabilities, took a grade-level written assessment. Some used accommodations during the testing. All the students shared key points both during their classroom activities and from their home projects. Besides sharing their experiences with one another, the children displayed their work for others to see outside their classroom and on a main bulletin board.

In addition to the many ways that O'Hearn teachers creatively integrated the arts and technology, they also adapted and utilized as UDL strategies for the entire class other programs that had initially been planned for individual students with disabilities. For example:

- Fifth-grade teachers selected and implemented for all students some of the behavior management procedures that were designed for students with attention deficit hyperactivity disorders (ADHD).
- To improve comprehension during reading lessons, third-grade teachers regularly utilized some strategies that were recommended as intensive interventions for students with specific learning disabilities.
- First-grade teachers taught the entire class helpful handwriting techniques from a program that was geared for students with fine-motor-control difficulties.
- The music teacher employed some of the dramatic expression and movement strategies that were promoted in music therapy for children with autism.
- Fourth-grade teachers presented graphic organizers to solve multiple-step math problems; these organizers were originally developed for students who struggled with organization and executive functioning.

Expanded Instructional Repertoire

Including students with disabilities forced us to diversify instructional strategies and to provide access to multileveled materials throughout the curricula. But standards did not change. Most students with disabilities were expected to achieve at or above the same rigorous levels as those expected of their non-disabled peers. This meant that we had to become very assertive about identifying and implementing appropriate support and accommodations. Only the children with intellectual disabilities had standards that were modified to lower levels according to their needs, and at the O'Hearn, these students still participated in general-content-area classes and school-wide activities.

Initially, we had turned to the arts, technology, specialized instruction, and UDL primarily to support our students with disabilities. What we discovered, though, was how important all these approaches were for enriching teaching and learning for all our students. In addition, it became easier and more natural for us to diversify strategies and materials for any student, including those who were advanced. With this expanded instructional repertoire, talented and gifted students (some of whom also had disabilities) began to thrive even more so at the O'Hearn. They, too, benefited tremendously from the arts, technology, and other innovative strategies and programs.

The efforts at organizing teaching and learning to help all O'Hearn children learn and succeed were definitely ongoing. Our staff members had to extend tremendous amounts of energy, and they demonstrated great flexibility and creativity. Sometimes, we used to say that we would try almost anything to help a child succeed—as long as it was humane and legal. We encountered many challenges, and not all of our interventions were as effective as we had hoped. Thus, we had to commit to keep assessing and trying different approaches and materials to determine what would work best. However, the steadfast vision of teaching and learning in a multi-abled community with many paths toward achievement and success served as the guiding star that would help make inclusive education beneficial to all.

4

SENSITIVITY WITH HIGH EXPECTATIONS

THE STUDENT'S CHALLENGE

"When are you going to kick me out of this school?"

These are the words that Alex screamed at me late one morning in November. It was his first day at the O'Hearn in our grade one class. He had already been "asked to leave" two other schools that fall (one charter school and one parochial school). His parents were involved in a heated custody dispute, and there were allegations of abuse. Alex's teacher had escorted him to the office because he had knocked over some tables and chairs after she had announced to the class that it was time to stop drawing, clean up, and move to another activity. I was well aware that it would have been fruitless to try to engage in a long conversation with Alex while he was so extremely upset. So I quickly spoke with his teacher, who needed to get back to the class, and suggested to Alex that he help himself to some water and look at the great books on the table in my office while I finished up my work.

A few moments later, I heard Alex take a little cup from the dispenser and fill it with water. Next, he started flipping through the colorful books that were on the table. I continued working on my talking computer. After about five minutes, Alex asked me about the noise coming from my computer, and I invited him over. I had found the distraction of the fast, robotic voice from my screen reader to be helpful in calming students who were agitated. Alex remarked that it was cool and asked if he could try it. I assured him that he could get a chance on it, but I told him about the following rule: Only students whose teachers had told me that the students had done some "good work" that day could use it.

Over the next couple of weeks, I had many conversations with Alex in my office. These occurred at least a couple of times each day and usually because he had engaged in some disruptive behavior (throwing, shouting, swearing, or flailing), and he needed some time-out. On many occasions, Alex would ask me, "When are you going to kick me out?" Being kicked out was what he expected, and it was also what his mother (who was currently seeing him only on weekends) kept reminding him would happen because he "didn't know how to behave."

We repeatedly told Alex that we didn't kick kids out of the O'Hearn and that we expected him, like the other students, to do good work and make a lot of progress. I also shared with Alex how some folks thought that I, his principal, should have been kicked out of school when I started losing my vision while I was a teacher and that they were wrong. This intrigued him, but even though he regularly heard our words of commitment to helping him, his disruptive behaviors continued. Although his teachers were untiring in welcoming him each morning and after each time-out, and although they worked hard to arrange activities in which they thought he could be most successful, we clearly needed some assistance in helping him make greater progress.

A behavior specialist from the district was contacted for support and came to observe the class and consult with us. We all agreed that Alex had significant emotional problems and that he, unfortunately, expected to fail and be punished. Although the class operated under a fairly successful positive behavior plan that stipulated rewards and consequences, Alex needed something more intensive and individually tailored. Alex's input was critical for his plan. Interestingly, he preferred going to the office, extra time on the computer, or playing with the math blocks over special rewards. Because of his emotional fragility and his experiences with and expectations of failure, the behavior specialist recommended that initially, Alex would only have to keep on task without disruptions for just fifteen minutes to receive a reward and that he should receive these rewards as frequently as possible throughout the day. Alex was also seeing a therapist on a weekly basis at a local health center. His father gave us permission to contact the therapist, who concurred with the behavior plan and communicated regularly with our teachers regarding his progress.

I believe that it is often easier for most people, including teachers and school staff, to be more sensitive, and to reach out with more kindness and warmth, to students with significant physical or intellectual disabilities than it is when dealing with students with emotional disorders. Physical and intellectual impairments are easier to understand and tend to elicit a greater desire to help. (There is, of course, a danger of being overly helpful to students with disabilities and not doing enough to maximize their independence and growth.) Becoming blind brought me into contact with many others who had a range of disabilities, and I learned to appreciate the tremendous diversity of characteristics. Even within the same disability group, there are many differences. Generalizations may be erroneous because each individual will have some specific interests and needs. In many ways, Alex required many more interventions and services than did the student in his class with Down syndrome and the student using a wheelchair. Like these students with more obvious disabilities, we would need to support Alex while we encouraged him to take as much responsibility as possible in terms of working hard and doing his best to learn and succeed.

Alex liked earning his rewards, and he started participating more appropriately in fifteen-minute stretches on a more regular basis. He often chose coming to the office as a positive reinforcement. Sometimes I was able to stop what I was doing to give him immediate attention, but sometimes I was engaged in a meeting or observing classrooms and so the secretary had to set a time later in the same day for a quick visit. Alex loved working on my talking computer with its robotic voice, and he occasionally wrote stories and completed assignments on it. Alex still had some slips and still had to spend some time-out both in the classroom and in other areas, including the office. Wherever his time-outs happened, efforts were made to make them short in duration and with minimal adult interactions. Before he could return to the classroom, he was usually responsible for drawing a picture, for writing a few sentences regarding the transgression, and for showing a willingness to make amends.

It was hard for some to accept Alex's getting a reward for what most of the other children were expected to do routinely without such special attention. Interestingly, Alex's young classmates recognized that he would sometimes (in their words) "get mad" and "be bad," which would upset some of them. With the guidance of the behavior specialist, the teachers simply explained that Alex was learning how to do things the right way, and it was clear that his classmates wanted him to succeed. Brilliantly, one of his teachers, who had been so patient with him, suggested that Alex could choose a different classmate each time to accompany him while he was experiencing (usually for just a few minutes) his special reward. His classmates actually started encouraging him and sometimes cheered when he was able to do his work and participate appropriately for the designated time. At first, these trial periods were set for just fifteen minutes. With more success and with his understanding, the expectations for good work and behaviors gradually increased to thirty minutes, then to one hour, and eventually to the entire morning or afternoon. Alex was making progress. He was making friends. Even his mother, who lost custody rights, admitted that he was "learning how to behave."

Alex made tremendous progress during the two years that he attended the O'Hearn. His participation and behavior during lessons and activities became mostly positive. Although he did not quite achieve proficiency on the district assessments, his scores were close to that level and his schoolwork was generally at grade level. Alex's teachers deserve much credit for the significant improvements that they helped him make, both academically and socially. Interestingly, Alex eventually stopped asking for the special rewards. Once he started experiencing and expecting more success, he preferred to stay with his classmates. The staff and I still needed to check in and talk with him frequently. He expressed how difficult it was for him to only see his mother in the occasional supervised visits stipulated by the custody agreement. Before he entered third grade, Alex and his father move out of state to be closer to his paternal grandparents. We heard from them periodically that first year, and it sounded as if he was doing fine. Eventually we lost contact with the family, but we felt hopeful and fairly confident that he would continue to do well. We believed his experience at the O'Hearn contributed greatly to his transformation.

THE PRINCIPAL'S CHALLENGE

Looking back, I recognize how I, too, as a person who had a disability, both needed and benefited from the sensitivity of others. In my early years of vision loss, I did not readily admit to others that I had some difficulties seeing, and this created some awkwardness for my family members, who were the only ones who knew that I was legally blind. I certainly could not expect strangers or drivers whom I encountered while walking on the sidewalks or crossing streets to be sensitive to my visual impairment if I were not alerting them with the use of a white cane. Because I could still see somewhat, I was reluctant and embarrassed to start using a cane. Not until I almost caused myself and my young son to be run over by a car that I did not notice coming out of the shadows on a noisy downtown street did things change for me. If I were going to stay active in my professional and family life, I could no longer pretend that I could see normally. I realized that I would finally have to "come out of the closet" about going blind.

I started using a white cane in the 1980s when walking in crowded areas and navigating around the school, where I had previously nervously tried to hide my impairment. Most teachers treated me pretty much the same (which is what I wanted), and after some initial surprise, my middle-school students acted as though it was no big deal. Initially, my own children found my white cane to be cool, but they were quickly much more interested in what we were going to have for dinner.

Being openly visually impaired, I very much appreciated the offers of rides from some colleagues and their willingness to assist with some tricky tasks like setting up the old film projector or filling in tiny boxes on administrative forms. However, I still had to prepare my lessons and teach a number of subjects. I still had to deal with students who worked hard and those who frequently fooled around. There were plenty of papers to correct and materials to read. As my vision decreased, the district accommodated me by providing a closed-circuit TV that enlarged and darkened print; a knowledgeable and patient technology specialist helped me learn how to use it and other adaptive equipment. With sensitivity and support from others, I was learning how to be a blind educator.

When I arrived at the O'Hearn in the summer of 1989 a few weeks before school opened, I was indeed fortunate to encounter a secretary and a custodian who were sensitive to the new principal who was blind. In addition to her regular responsibilities for dealing with attendance, payroll, operational reports, supplies, phone calls, and all visitors, the school secretary spent extra time helping me with many tasks, including the print mail and correspondence. The custodian was gracious in helping me locate items and offering me rides when needed. Recognizing their extra efforts, I tried to show my appreciation and to help them out when I could. Thus, every day, I spent a little time answering the phone or opening the front door and likewise moving around furniture and changing the five-gallon water bottles. It was great to be able to contribute and help out even in little ways.

Over the years, other staff, parents, students, and colleagues regularly showed wonderful sensitivity around my blindness. This was most evident to me in the little things such as pointing out when there were some special treats to eat, describing drawings orally to me, and reading or summarizing student work that we were assessing. Receiving so many acts of kindness encouraged me to work even harder. Every day, students and staff reminded me of the importance of being attentive to individual needs at the same time that I was responsible for encouraging them to learn or teach at the highest possible levels.

IMPLICATIONS FOR THE SCHOOL

All students, and not just those with disabilities, deserve to be treated with appropriate sensitivity by teachers and school staff. Every child, at some time or another, experiences some discomfort dealing with health issues, frustrations at school, interpersonal relations, or family squabbles. Some children face the additional challenges of the loss of a close family member, abuse, or extreme poverty. This meant that O'Hearn staff did not always treat students the same. At one time or another, every student needs, deserves, and should receive extra support, whether the child has disabilities or not.

I remember responding to a parent who was upset because a lunch monitor who supervised students in the cafeteria and at recess had bought and served a birthday cake at lunch for one student in the class, but had not volunteered to do the same for her daughter, whose birthday would be the following week. The birthday boy happened to live in a family that was dealing with significant problems, and he exhibited serious emotional difficulties. The week before his tenth birthday, he had written in his journal about how his parents never did much for his birthday and how much this bothered him. Since there were no religious reasons for not celebrating his birthday, staff wanted to cheer him up by serving a cake and singing a song to him at lunch with the entire class. Without going into all the details of the boy's family situation, I explained to the protesting parent that her daughter had also eaten some cake and participated in the short party and that she was fortunate to live in a family that was able to provide treats and gifts at birthdays.

The parent was still concerned that the school was not demonstrating the principle of equal treatment for all. I pointed out to her that she was, in part, correct. At the O'Hearn, we strived to be sensitive to and maintain high expectations for everyone, and this meant that sometimes, we had to respond to students' needs differently. Subsequently, I reminded the parent how her daughter had received and benefited from extra tutoring offered at no cost during our after-school program. This was needed to help her improve in mathematics, which was a growth area for her. I then explained how I, as a blind principal, also needed and received some unique support that other principals did not need.

Including students with significant disabilities at the O'Hearn forced the entire school community to be more sensitive about individual needs. Being around children who had major difficulties opening doors, holding a spoon, reading almost any words, and wiping away their own drool prompted others to get involved. It was particularly wonderful to witness how naturally so many children graciously offered appropriate support. Inclusion provided ample opportunities to practice being helpful and compassionate and, as a result, contributed to each child's own well-being.

Of course, sometimes the students, and occasionally some staff, provided too much help and did not allow the students with the most apparent disabilities to be as independent as possible. In addition to having needs, students with disabilities also had potential, and it was equally important for us at the O'Hearn to be aware of this potential to encourage and support these students and maximize their development. This meant that we sometimes had to explain to students' parents and staff how it was sometimes best not to provide too much assistance and to let the individuals with disabilities work on a task more independently.

In addition to being sensitive, it was equally important for us to demonstrate high expectations by holding students with disabilities accountable for completing work and following rules for which they were capable. For example:

- A kindergarten student with cerebral palsy refused to draw a circle and had to stay in for recess until he tried to do his best using the cushion under his left arm and the special grip around the crayon that the teachers had prepared for him.
- A third-grade student with Down syndrome who wasted a lot of time looking around the room despite the teacher's many attempts at redirection had to stay after school to finish writing a story that should have been completed in class.

- A second-grade boy with autism snatched a book away from a classmate rather than asking for it using his words needed to go to the time-out corner and practice an apology.
- A blind fourth-grade student who submitted her social studies report after the deadline without having asked for an extension lost some points on her grade for its being late.
- A fifth-grade girl who drove her electric wheelchair too quickly down the left side of the corridor to race ahead of her classmates needed to go to the back of the line, though she did so with a big smile for having gotten "busted."

Promoting sensitivity with high expectations posed some challenges that in a few rare cases, we could not always resolve. I remember a second-grader who, like Alex, had experienced some trauma. When she enrolled at the O'Hearn, she was in the custody of her aunt because her parents had been found guilty of neglect and abuse. The girl also had some mild delays, but everyone thought that she should be doing much more than she was in literacy and math. Unfortunately, much of the time when we encouraged her to follow the class routines and participate with her peers, especially on academic tasks, she either crawled under her desk and refused to work or became so agitated that it escalated into a tantrum. These spells occurred up to three times a day and occasionally lasted over thirty minutes.

In accordance with the girl's IEP, the teachers would try to calm her down and to make sure that her next assignments would be relatively easy and enjoyable. Increasingly, though, she started thrashing and screaming and even banging her head. When these self-injurious and disruptive behaviors occurred, the teachers rushed to protect her and called for support to escort her to the office or to another quieter area of the school. With the aunt's permission, we spoke with the girl's doctors. We invited experts in behavior support to visit our school. We even utilized the city's emergency response team. Everyone agreed that her classroom teachers were supportive and were trying all the recommended techniques to help her participate and do some modified assignments. The only new suggestion that we received from the experts (and for reasons of space and privacy, we did not follow the suggestion) was that we put a padded box in the office so that she could go in there and bang safely in the midst of her tantrums. Although the staff and the girl's family had developed a positive relationship and hoped that she could remain at the O'Hearn, we recognized that inclusion was not working for her at that time in her life. The teachers, family, and outside supporters met together at frequent IEP meetings. Eventually, they recommended a different placement, and the girl was assigned to a separate school with small classes and with intensive therapeutic services.

Most students with disabilities at the O'Hearn, though, including those with emotional disorders, did make substantial progress. Because we were an inclusive school, staff and students were well aware of the extra consideration and support that many children regularly received. The adults at the school also witnessed how these same students were challenged to participate and do their best. Both compassion and achievement were important. It was more common and comfortable at our inclusive school for all students to express needs and expect both to receive support and to provide it to others. There were also far fewer excuses for not participating in activities or for not completing tasks. Everyone was expected to work hard and to make progress. Everyone was expected to contribute and to follow basic rules. Sensitivity with high expectations created an inclusive learning environment in which abilities could be developed and children could flourish.

5

✦

ORGANIZATION AND PLANNING FOR SUCCESS

THE STUDENT'S CHALLENGE

"You are going to have a tough year with her."

These are the words that a parent blurted to me on the opening day of school in front of her daughter and around others who were mingling outside by the main entrance. Laurie was ten years old and entering our grade four. She had transferred from another Boston school where, according to the mother, she had "been kept back and done miserably." I quickly assured Laurie that she was going to learn a lot and have a good year at the O'Hearn. Laurie said that she felt sick and wanted to go home. I discreetly spoke with her teacher, who went over to Laurie, and after some positive and welcoming words, encouraged the girl to enter the building.

As documented in her Individualized Education Program (IEP), Laurie had significant specific learning disabilities and attention deficit hyperactivity disorders (ADHD). We soon observed that she had major difficulties decoding words and that her oral reading fluency was laborious. She demonstrated difficulty sitting still and focusing. It also became apparent that she was quite disorganized and spent lots of time locating items and getting ready at transitions.

The teachers assigned Laurie to sit at a desk that was near a student who had significant intellectual and physical disabilities. Laurie reacted positively to this arrangement and eagerly volunteered to push this boy around in his wheelchair at transition times. She seemed to really enjoy arts class and was excited about any opportunity to draw. At recess, she ran freely and with speed. Although somewhat timid at first, she had generally positive interactions with her peers, and she participated eagerly in projects that involved a lot of activity. When it was time to sit and complete assignments independently such as reading a book or writing an essay, Laurie became extremely anxious. She took a long time getting ready, she fidgeted a great deal, and sometimes she even acted as if she were in pain. Clearly, we would have to plan teaching and learning quite differently to help her make progress and experience success.

Laurie needed to improve in many areas, and her teachers felt that her becoming more organized was an important first step. Her desk was generally messy, with things scattered all over it. It took her a long time to find what she needed and get started on her work. She sometimes gave the appearance of being discombobulated. Fortunately, her teachers had lots of experience helping other students with organization issues. These students, including those with significant autism and intellectual disabilities, had benefited from clear systems and routines. The teachers asked Laurie to select different-colored folders in which she could keep papers and materials for each of her subjects. Using plastic dividers inside her desk, she organized her pencils, eraser, pens, crayons, folders, and books in designated compartments. She was responsible for making sure that these items were in order both before the midday lunch and recess period and before leaving to go home. Using words and graphics designed with a computer, she had a laminated copy of her daily schedule on her desk, in her book bag, and inside her major subject folders. Initially, the teachers gave Laurie cues slightly before the major transition times to help facilitate her getting ready for the next task. They also sent home a special homework folder with an accompanying simple checklist that her mother needed to sign every day.

Laurie needed other interventions to accelerate her progress and to work more at grade level. Like some other students with print disabilities at the O'Hearn, she started using Kurzweil software on a daily basis to help herself gain access to, and respond to, text that she otherwise could not read. Kurzweil is a software program that allows students to both see and hear text that can be scanned or downloaded onto a computer. The program provides many tools that can be employed to facilitate reading and writing. Laurie really enjoyed how she could set both the quality and the speed of the voice output. For the first time, decoding was not an impediment for her learning. She was able to keep up with and comprehend all the grade-level reading assignments. Using the word prediction and other graphic organizer features, she was also able to write better-developed essays and compositions. The school provided her with a thumb-drive version of the software to help her continue reading and complete her assignments at home. Because the Kurzweil program was listed by the state as an approved accommodation, Laurie utilized the program with both standardized and with teacher-prepared assessments. Kurzweil software helped Laurie make much progress and develop confidence.

Because of her difficulties with decoding, Laurie received specialized instruction in a rules-based and multisensory phonics program. A teacher with expertise in this program tutored her before school three times per week, and Laurie had opportunities to practice the new strategies during some of her regular English/language arts classes and at home. Laurie demonstrated modest improvements in both accuracy and speed while decoding printed text, but she still labored noticeably when reading challenging material. This frustrated her, and without the accommodations, she clearly read less and did not comprehend as much. Reading with the text and speech features provided by the Kurzweil program was definitely Laurie's most efficient way to read.

In terms of her ADHD, Laurie previously tried some medication under the direction of her pediatrician. Her parents maintained that although the medication helped her focus a bit more, it also caused her to be more lethargic, and so they usually chose not to give it to her. Having opportunities to move around were critical for Laurie. She enjoyed the before-school kickball game in the back courtyard and ran and played a great deal during the daily recess. She exuded a lot of energy during the school's excellent movement class, which she took twice a week. Laurie also benefited from a variety of props, including special seat cushions, stools, and squeezable objects. Using these helped her to focus better while moving quietly without distracting others. When there was no outdoor recess because of weather conditions, Laurie asked to go to the sensory motor area—a request that we tried to accommodate. She enjoyed using the swing, exercise balls, and the balancing and stretching equipment. All these activities helped prepare Laurie to do better work.

Laurie began to truly flourish in the arts. The visual arts teacher at our school quickly recognized Laurie's abilities to capture details and share insights in both drawings and paintings. Laurie's classroom teachers encouraged her to embellish her written assignments with related artwork. Her intricate depictions of characters, scenes, and events attracted much praise from classmates. The practice of integrating arts throughout the curricula at the O'Hearn certainly benefited Laurie. She was more motivated and engaged in all her classes whenever she had opportunities to use the arts.

Laurie's disabilities did not go away, but she became more comfortable in class even with assignments that were challenging. She still needed the accommodations and specialized instruction with reading and writing, and for her, reminders and guidance around organization were still a necessity. She also needed the continued, regular opportunities to exercise and to engage in the arts. Because Laurie's teachers and parents collaborated so well together and because she was such a hard worker, Laurie made steady progress. With accommodations providing text and speech, she scored at the proficient level on the state assessments. Her artwork was displayed not only in the school but also at special exhibits in the community. After graduating from the O'Hearn, Laurie attended a nearby middle school and continued to do well. For high school, she auditioned for, and was accepted at, a district school that had a major focus on the arts. We were thrilled when Laurie decided to volunteer a couple of times each week in our after-school program. She proved to be a tremendous help assisting younger students with art and even with their assignments involving writing.

THE PRINCIPAL'S CHALLENGE

I experienced my own anxieties and frustrations when I started losing my vision. Simple things like finding items, getting phone numbers, and reading and processing correspondence sometimes became major ordeals. If I had not spent the time and learned how to organize around what had previously been the simplest of tasks <u>with sight</u>, I could not have functioned physically or emotionally as the O'Hearn's principal. There were literally hundreds of details, requests, and suggestions that I had to deal with on a daily basis, and I needed to handle these quickly, efficiently, and without sight.

Most of my communications with adults as principal happened by speaking with them either directly in person or over the phone. However, there were many times each day that I needed to rely on writing to convey a particular message or to ask specific questions. Sometimes, I would use my computer and its talking screen reader to send an e-mail. Other times, I would use my Braille note taker, which I could touch or listen to in order to recall specific details. (I would input data onto my Braille note taker by using the six keys that represented the six dots of each Braille cell, and I would retrieve the data either by feeling the dots on a refreshable Braille display or by listening to its robotic voice.) Sometimes, it was quicker and more efficient for me to use a marker and pad of paper so that I could either directly hand-deliver the message with some additional comments or just put the simple written note (e.g., "see me about . . . " or "call Maria's mom about . . .") in a staff member's mailbox. Students frequently asked me how I, a blind person, could write a note. I would demonstrate this by covering their eyes and asking them to write their names. Usually, they were pleasantly surprised to see how they accomplished this as legibly as I could write my own short messages.

Accessing phone numbers quickly was also important. Blind people can use the 411 information code at no charge. But many numbers of individuals and extensions of administrative offices are not listed. Most of the numbers that I called regularly I just memorized. Other numbers I stored both on my computer and on my Braille note taker. Some numbers, though, were written on the students' emergency cards or on School Department directories, and I would ask an adult and, sometimes, a student to read them to me.

Reading and processing written correspondence was a bit trickier. The school secretary who was busy answering phone calls, welcoming all visitors, completing administrative reports, and dealing with constant requests, spent about ten to fifteen minutes with me each day quickly processing the general mail and print documents sent by the School Department. Over the years, the amount of papers that we had to review diminished, because more was sent electronically (which I could handle more independently with my screen reader) and because the secretary would recycle most of the junk mail before she and I even met. Because of the relatively short time that we had together, she would primarily just read out loud the titles and subjects of the documents, and then we would quickly decide where to put the material. Some would go in a to-do pile, which I would have to examine more carefully with another helper whom I would recruit later that same day. Some would go into the well-organized office files, some would go (sometimes with a short note) in the mailbox of the staff member who needed to deal with it, and much would be recycled. What I could not afford to do, though, was to let the materials pile up, and I needed to take advantage of the various sources of support when I had them. That's why my desk always appeared to be orderly and not at all cluttered. There were always some jealous principal colleagues who wanted to know how I could manage to keep such a relatively empty desk. Going blind had certainly forced that issue.

To function efficiently as a principal, I had to conscientiously organize and prepare. I had to know exactly where I put things if I was going to quickly find them again. My white cane was standing in the paper recycle box, my pads of paper were in the bottom right-hand drawer, and the list of phone numbers for the various bus yards was in the wire basket on the right-hand corner of my desk. The stapler was next to the phone on the top left corner of my desk. When others borrowed any of these items, they knew it was important that they return them to the same location. After wasting lots of time trying to find the scissors, which never seemed to make it back to the top middle drawer, I learned that tying a large, pink ribbon to one of the handles helped others remember to return them when they finished.

Perhaps my systems of organization may seem a bit obsessive, and I definitely would not have used all the same techniques if I had been sighted, but they worked for me and helped me get things done. Any good principal needs to be organized. The work is demanding, and its pace is relentless. Having to be more organized made me more efficient. It was also good role modeling.

IMPLICATIONS FOR THE SCHOOL

Because the O'Hearn included many so students with disabilities, the entire staff and I had to be more conscious about organization to meet the students' diverse needs. The following extra preparations that were essential for some individuals also proved beneficial for others without disabilities:

- Specially designed schedules with words, graphics, or Velcro-backed icons to help students make a smooth transition from one activity to another
- Adapted notebooks, dividers, and containers to store and access students' classroom materials
- Graphic organizers to help students with assignments like solving multiple-step math problems or writing a five-paragraph persuasive essay
- Visual charts describing the routines for eating in the cafeteria or for cleaning up in their rooms
- Personalized charts showing students how to proceed during a science experiment
- Other specialized cues to redirect students to appropriate work

Because the O'Hearn served children with disabilities, all the staff members needed to spend extra time planning and organizing for their classes and rooms. These additional efforts helped staff become more effective teachers for every student. For example:

- Teachers had to be more conscious about communicating lesson objectives in ways that all students clearly understood what they were expected to know and to do. Using concise language and some creativity, teachers needed to share class objectives orally, on the blackboard, and sometimes on specially designed charts.

- Staff needed to set clear procedures and routines that minimized confusion. These covered daily occurrences such as how to ask questions in class, how to line up to go to the bathroom, what to do after finishing work, and how to get help or respond to classmates during lessons.
- Staff had to create better systems for storing and distributing materials and adapted devices so that they could be quickly accessed. This meant that there needed to be more space and less clutter for students to easily maneuver, and materials needed to be stored and labeled appropriately for children.
- Teachers had to prepare more for universal design for learning (UDL). For every standard, they needed to arrange multiple ways that students could access information, be engaged, and show understanding. They also had to provide materials for students working at varying skill levels.
- Teachers needed to pace themselves to ensure that they were on track to cover entire units, to analyze and record assessment data, and to prepare for IEP and other meetings in a timely manner.

As principal of an inclusive school, I was responsible for organizing staff and class schedules in ways that maximized teaching and learning for everyone at the same time that I had to ensure that students with disabilities were receiving appropriate support. For example, given the students' varying needs, I had to allow for a little more time for transitions between classrooms and other areas of the school. I also needed to check that therapists were assisting students at appropriate times and, as much as possible, in classrooms or other natural environments. The therapist also needed designated times to consult with homeroom teachers. Scheduling was another priority for paraprofessionals; I sometimes had to juggle schedules so that they could assist the students with the most significant needs. What's more, I needed to set aside some times that teachers could participate in common planning and in collaborative observations. Finally, I had to facilitate more time for meetings with parents whose children had more complex issues.

Over the years, I learned how accountability and follow-through were critical aspects of my responsibilities. Otherwise, the best-organized plans were flawed, and teaching and learning usually suffered. I established many routines that happened on different time intervals so that I could stay informed and to ensure student progress. For example:

- At least a few times every year, usually around report card distribution, I met with staff to review each student's achievement and progress. The district provided increasing amounts of data to help with this process. Obviously, this review happened more frequently when there were problems.
- Once a month, I met with the O'Hearn's Math Leadership Team (MLT) to discuss our progress teaching math, with the Instructional Leadership Team (ILT) to examine literacy and the implementation of other curricula priorities, and with the School Site Council (SSC). (See details on the SSC below.) Most months, I also met either with members of the O'Hearn Family Outreach Program or with the O'Hearn School Parent Council.

(See more information about these groups and other parent collaboration in chapter 8.) Occasionally, I met with the Faculty Senate, which discusses concerns among the teaching staff.

- I usually met weekly with cross-grade-level teams of teachers, lunch staff, after-school coordinators, and key outside consultants.

- Most importantly, on a daily basis, I needed to check in with all staff, visit all classrooms during instructional time, respond to e-mail and phone messages, monitor arrival and dismissal time, oversee lunches and recess, communicate with enthusiasm, and be emotionally prepared for pleasant and not-so-pleasant surprises. In addition, I kept daily lists of names of students and staff with whom I needed to connect. Some needed to give me updates on particular issues. Others had to submit written assignments or reports. I believe that it was particularly critical to follow through on student discipline. Otherwise, our rules and consequences would have been like window dressing. Being organized was critical.

School Site Council (SSC)

In our first year of implementing inclusive education, the O'Hearn established a School Site Council. The SSC became the organization responsible for making recommendations on programs, budget, and new personnel according to guidelines set by the Boston School Department. Six representatives were selected by parents, five representatives were selected by staff, and I was the administrator representative. The monthly SSC meetings were open, and other staff members and parents usually attended. On most of the matters discussed, we made decisions by consensus, but on some issues, we needed to vote and followed the majority rule.

One ground rule that we established as a council was that we did not publicly talk about individual students, staff, or family members if it were in a critical or pejorative way. Here is how the rule played out:

- We could talk about improving the situation in the cafeteria, but not about an individual lunch monitor who some thought was unpleasant.
- We could discuss implementing the new math program, but not the teacher who someone thought needed more training.
- We could describe the overall growth areas for students on the writing assessments, but not the names of the students with the lowest scores.
- We could identify guidelines for fair play at recess, but not the students who frequently got into trouble.
- We could brainstorm ways of increasing parent attendance at the upcoming teacher-parent conferences, but not the situations of particular families experiencing major problems.

For each of these situations, there were opportunities for parents to talk privately with me about particular concerns. If parents were not satisfied with the way that I handled the situations, there were other School Department and city officials with whom they could talk. However, I felt that dealing publicly about growth areas for individual children, staff, or parents would have been divisive to our school and detrimental to positive collaboration.

One of the first orders of business for the SCC was to develop a mission statement. Although the statement continued to evolve and be refined over the years, the basic tenets remained the same:

- We were committed to help all children learn and succeed at high levels. "All" encompassed students from early childhood through grade five and students from diverse ethnic, linguistic, and ability backgrounds.
- We celebrated being an inclusive school. "Inclusive" meant that students involved in regular education; students with mild, moderate, and significant disabilities; and students considered talented and gifted would learn together and from each other.
- Teachers and support staff collaborated to serve all students. "Support staff" referred to everyone at the O'Hearn who, along with the teachers, was responsible for providing services in the context of team teaching and inclusion.
- Family involvement, the arts, and technology were also prioritized at the O'Hearn in the mission statement, with implications for all students and staff.

Another important task of the SCC was the drafting of a new, inclusive teacher job description. When inclusion began at the O'Hearn in September 1989, all classroom teachers who had worked there previously and who had elected to stay acknowledged that they were also going to work with students who had a range of disabilities. However, none of the teachers who were assigned that year to the O'Hearn in enrichment areas such as art, music, and physical education had been aware of the inclusion. Moreover, some of the therapists designated to work at the O'Hearn had been accustomed to providing most of their services to students in separate rooms, apart from the regular classrooms. Finally, any future teacher openings at the O'Hearn could be filled by persons transferring from another Boston school without the teacher's making any commitment to inclusion. Parents of students with disabilities were very concerned that some staff might not have the necessary will or skills to deal with their children. Likewise, the staff and I did not expect—nor did we think it possible—that the special education teachers should be the only ones responsible for dealing with the large numbers of students with disabilities, and we recognized how the participation and collaboration of all staff around inclusion would be key for success.

At that time, the existing job descriptions of special education and regular education teachers in the Boston Public Schools were quite different. Because we believed that those job descriptions were not appropriate for our inclusive program, we drafted our own. Basically, we combined many of the tasks from both the general-education and the special education job descriptions so that all teachers, specialists, therapists, and paraprofessionals were responsible for serving all students in an inclusive environment, even though these educators also specialized in one particular area. In addition, we explicitly stated that all teaching staff who worked at the O'Hearn were responsible for helping students with disabilities with accommodations or modifications to access curricula, with specialized equipment and assistive technology, and with the activities of daily living, including toileting.

Given our inclusive program and the unique needs of many of our students, and given the united and strong advocacy of parents and staff, both the Boston School Department and the Boston Teachers Union accepted our expanded job description. We still had to ensure that teachers had at least one of the necessary certification areas, but they were also all expected to assist students with disabilities in their inclusive classrooms.

What was transformative about this opportunity was that the O'Hearn had effectively been granted much more autonomy for selecting all new teachers and paraprofessionals. Subsequently, we utilized an open posting process and a personnel subcommittee to advertise staff vacancies and to interview candidates. As long as the applicants met the certification requirements, we at the O'Hearn had been granted the power to determine if they were also committed and skillful enough to work with students with a wide range of abilities in inclusive classrooms. This control over the selection of all new teaching staff was a critical factor in the school's future overall success, which probably would not have occurred without the inclusion of students with significant disabilities. One might have thought that we would be limiting ourselves by adding extra requirements to teachers' job descriptions. On the contrary, the number of applicants for each job opening increased dramatically, and we were able to select many excellent new staff from both within and outside the school district.

The O'Hearn School Site Council addressed many other issues over the years. These included our yearly whole-school improvement plans; the yearly budget; a mandatory school-uniform policy; the hiring of a dance/movement teacher instead of a physical education teacher; guidelines for school-wide events; fund-raising activities; grant applications; and the design and building of a playground for our younger children.

All of the organization and planning that occurred at the O'Hearn required a tremendous amount of work. The more that the school community collaborated on it, the less daunting it became. However, each year and each day brought some new variations. Organization and planning had to be ongoing, and including students with disabilities necessitated more flexibility and adjustments. The extra efforts at organization—extra because of our desire for inclusion of students with disabilities—helped us build a stronger and more effective school community for everyone. We became more conscientious about determining all students' needs, and we collaborated more to plan and implement programs and strategies to ensure all students' success.

6

❖

COLLABORATION AMONG STAFF

THE STUDENT'S CHALLENGE

"What are you going to do with Rayba?"

This was the question justifiably posed to staff by a parent leader whose son Juan was a classmate of Rayba's in the first grade. Rayba was an energetic seven-year-old girl with Down syndrome. She had started as a three-year-old in our inclusive early-childhood class. She was accustomed to participating in a large group and had made progress in some areas. Because of her disability, though, her developmental level was closer to that of a much younger child. Over the previous month, staff and parents had observed how Rayba had started exhibiting much more defiance and negativity, in a way somewhat similar to typical children at the "terrible twos" developmental stage. Unfortunately, she had just thrown a block at Juan, and it had knocked out one of his front teeth. Although everyone recognized that Rayba had not intentionally hurt Juan—in fact, he was probably one of her favorite classmates—her increasingly disruptive and potentially dangerous behavior needed to change. The teachers tried to deal with her outbursts by using a number of creative strategies, but very little improvement was evident.

The school community came together to deal with the situation. Our goal was simple: to figure out what the staff could do to help Rayba become a better learner and behave better in class. It was determined that ten adults should be involved with this problem-solving group: Rayba's mother, a special education teacher, a general education teacher, a paraprofessional, a speech therapist, an occupational therapist, a physical therapist, a behavior specialist working with the district, a special education coordinator, and me. Arranging for a meeting in which all ten persons could be present during school hours was challenging and required some coverage, but we made it happen.

As a result of this initial meeting, the group agreed that a number of recommendations needed to be implemented. First, we made a commitment that for the time being, an adult would always be sitting next to Rayba. The adult was responsible for helping her keep on task and for stopping her from throwing objects or flailing at people, even if it meant physically redirecting her. A paraprofessional who previously worked mainly with a few other students was designated as the primary person responsible for this continuous supervision, but other staff, including therapists and teachers, took their turns.

Second, we made a commitment to provide Rayba with tasks that were simpler to master as well as engaging. Her assignments were carefully designed and adapted by teachers and therapists with the goal of minimizing frustration and maximizing success.

Third, we committed to provide Rayba with more frequent breaks and opportunities to go for a walk or to the sensory motor area if we noticed that she was getting "antsy." The adult who was with her at the time was responsible for implementing this. Sometimes these breaks occurred on schedule, and sometimes spontaneously, according to need.

Fourth, we made a commitment to provide a tremendous amount of positive reinforcement for both good work and appropriate behaviors. Rayba enjoyed oral praise, stickers, hugs, and the opportunity to choose special activities. Although adults were still primarily responsible for orchestrating these rewards, Rayba loved it when other children noticed her efforts and were involved in the positive reinforcements.

As a result of the implementation of these recommendations and the ongoing meetings mostly among staff but sometimes with her mother, Rayba demonstrated slow but steady improvements. Over the next few months, she developed into a student who worked a little harder in class and who usually interacted positively with peers. Her plan was continuously adjusted. Gradually, we reduced the time that adults were directly working with her, we increased the level of difficulty of her assignments, and we diminished both the number of her breaks and the frequency of her reinforcements. However, in each of these four areas, Rayba continued to receive special considerations and the staff continued to meet to discuss how to help her make even greater improvements.

The most significant factor in both the planning and the implementation of strategies to assist Rayba at the O'Hearn was that it was a team effort. There was no way that any one person could have designed and implemented all her support. Even though many of the same adults could have individually conceived and tried out similar ideas, their collective wisdom and efforts made the outcomes for Rayba much more successful. This level of collaboration necessitated a great deal of scheduling and prioritizing of time. It required that decisions be based on what the group, and not any one individual, believed was most appropriate. It also required a great deal of follow-through and continuous refinements.

Unfortunately, even with the tremendous efforts at collaboration and providing support, not every child at the O'Hearn performed the way that we had hoped. Over the years, there were a few students with disabilities who did not make sufficient improvements and who were recommended for more restrictive settings. These decisions usually involved students who had significant emotional disorders or mental health issues and who were overly distracted being in a large class or who continued to act in ways that were injurious to themselves or others. Despite the fact that some progress had been made, the IEP teams of these few students believed that a small, substantially separate classroom or a separate day school or residential school for students with similar disabilities was necessary and more appropriate. Most students who exhibited challenging behaviors at the O'Hearn, though, did make significant progress. Structured routines, hard work, skillful interventions, and extensive staff collaboration were critical factors in these students' improvements.

As for Rayba, she developed skills and learned to interact much more pleasantly and cooperatively with others. Her teachers continued to modify the skill level of her assignments, and they recognized how lots of praise and occasional hugs worked wonders. By the fifth grade, her abilities to read, write, and compute progressed to a level typical of a beginning grade-one student. This was a major achievement, given her cognitive delays. Rayba also participated eagerly in classroom and school-wide activities, and she tried much harder to complete her work.

Upon leaving the school, Rayba was assigned to a middle school that had a few inclusive classrooms, where she continued to make progress. Subsequently, because at that time there were no inclusive options in Boston for students with intellectual disabilities at the high school level, she enrolled in a school that offered a prevocational cluster program. When she turned twenty-two, she stayed at home, living with her parents and grandmother, but she joined a day program that offered supported work opportunities. The program director described Rayba as a good and cooperative worker.

THE PRINCIPAL'S CHALLENGE

As principal, I had the responsibility to establish a positive and productive working environment for everyone. Each day, I tried to greet all fifty-five full and part-time staff members and to check in with them to determine if there were any major needs. The staff felt comfortable communicating with me and did so frequently, mostly by talking with me directly and sometimes via e-mail. Most conversations were pleasant, respectful, and constructive. Although I could not radically alter the staff's primary jobs, I always offered encouragement and, whenever possible, provided any requested support.

It was also my responsibility as principal to supervise the staff, and because of blindness, a few things were trickier for me. I could no longer ascertain the quality of classroom charts, the cleanliness of the cafeteria floor, or the quality of support provided to a nonverbal student by vision alone. Although it was never my intent nor style to micromanage how the staff completed these and the myriad of other tasks, it was my job to ensure that everything was done well.

Being blind, I needed to collaborate with others more and utilize their insights to be better informed. In some ways, asking staff, students, and sometimes family members to describe how things were going gave me different perspectives on many important tasks. The bottom line, though, was always around the children and their performance. Students had to make continuous progress, and with the enactment of federal and state legislation, they had to achieve at increasingly rigorous levels. Every staff member at the O'Hearn, either directly or indirectly, had specific responsibilities that would affect how students would learn and succeed.

As the school's only administrator, I was charged with ensuring students' academic achievement as a primary goal for everyone. The district and state set clear standards and provided varying assessments that had to be followed. I needed to regularly review student progress either as it related to those standards or, for students with intellectual disabilities, as it related to the modified standards recommended by their IEP teams. Being blind, I probably communicated more directly with teachers about their students' work and about students' achievement and growth areas. I believe that these extra face-to-face conversations not only were very informative, but also provided more opportunities to discuss possible strategies for making improvements.

Early on, I recognized that we were not going to be successful with inclusion unless staff worked together and shared ideas cooperatively and effectively. The district had established general expectations regarding professional collaboration, and we developed additional guidelines necessary for including students with disabilities. Because I visited classrooms regularly and connected with all the O'Hearn staff each day, I had a fairly good understanding of how they were working with each other. There was, of course, an occasional disagreement among staff—such as the best time and ways to provide specific interventions. When there were differences of opinion, I encouraged the staff to try to speak directly with others about the situation while focusing on what was best for the students. This usually was sufficient, but occasionally, we needed to set up meetings with the individuals involved to clarify how services for children should happen.

In addition, staff members sometimes failed to demonstrate the levels of performance and conduct that I considered acceptable. When these situations occurred, I tried to deal with them directly. With appropriate guidance and support, most individuals made the necessary changes. Some needed more explicit directives such as requests to start lessons on time, to follow the curriculum, to share more at staff meetings, and to provide the appropriate accommodations. During these conversations with the staff member, I tried to clearly communicate how the required areas for improvement were related to the person's job description and to the school's overall mission of helping students learn and succeed. Over my twenty years at the O'Hearn, there were just a few individuals who, despite various interventions, still did not progress adequately. Like other principals, I usually sought advice from staff at the central office in the district about addressing these situations. Following the procedures established by the Boston Public Schools for staff evaluation and employee discipline, I was involved with removing a small number of staff from working at the school and some from even working anywhere in the district.

Indeed, sometimes it would have been easier to handle the staff regarding particular issues if I had had normal vision.

However, blindness did not keep me from taking actions. For example, I once gave a teacher an "unsatisfactory" on the item "appearance and demeanor," which appeared in that year's evaluation form. I explained to her that I usually heard her greeting children with a flat voice and a lack of enthusiasm. I suggested that she smile more and be more cheerful, and I demonstrated specific expressions and tones that I thought she could use. Similarly, another time, I had to talk with a young student teacher regarding her attire. A couple of female staff members had spoken with her about clothes that they believed were a bit too revealing. After I overheard some boys talking about her appearance in great detail, I shared some of the comments with her and told her that it would be wiser to dress in ways that were not so distracting.

My hearing helped me out in other ways. I set up a meeting with a paraprofessional who was frequently late when it was the day for her morning bus duty. She wondered whether sometimes she was there on time but perhaps I did not always notice her. I told her that it was unlikely that I had not heard her "sweet" voice, but to be sure that I did not miss her, she should always come over and greet me as soon as she arrived at the entrance area. Another teacher frequently took too much time locating student records and journals whenever I needed to discuss them with her. I suggested that if she reduced the piles that I heard her moving around on the desk and if she organized materials better, then things would probably be easier for her and much more efficient.

Other senses provide plenty of information if you pay attention to them. I once informed a substitute custodian that he did a poor job cleaning the floor. Not only did I know this from hearing people's comments, but I could feel the stickiness with my feet. I asked him if he needed any assistance in making the floor acceptable before he left to go home. Sometimes I had to direct bus drivers waiting in line outside before dismissal to move their buses forward and closer together so that all buses could get off the main street. I determined whether there was too much space between buses by tapping the sides of the vehicles with my cane. And once, before school started, I told a staff member that he needed to go home and get some sleep. According to what others had told me and what I could smell, he evidently was still recuperating from drinking too much the night before.

I took cues from the students as well. Remembering children's comments, for example, I occasionally informed teachers that some of their students could not clearly decipher what they had written on the board.

As the preceding examples show, most of my conversations and interactions with staff had little to do with eyesight. My belief about staff performance was that everyone, including myself, always had some areas for growth and improvements. It was my responsibility to ask questions, to listen to others' ideas and concerns, to offer support, and, when necessary, to suggest changes. Sometimes I had time to think about the issues, but other times I had to make decisions quickly. Looking back, there were definitely times when I could have handled particular situations better, but not responding and not dealing with them would have been worse.

Overall, most O'Hearn staff were clearly exemplary in the day-to-day performance of their jobs. I expressed appreciation for their terrific contributions, but probably should have done so even more. Mediocrity was really not an option for us. Having so many students with disabilities and having to collaborate with so many others to help students learn and succeed required staff to be more skillful and flexible than would have been necessary in other settings. Inclusion at the O'Hearn certainly forced staff to work harder and to collaborate more. Going blind had that same impact on me.

IMPLICATIONS FOR THE SCHOOL

While the adults at the O'Hearn were working together on inclusion on a daily basis, the leadership team of the Boston Public Schools initiated in the late 1990s a system-wide campaign promoting greater staff collaboration. The leaders maintained that schools that developed professional learning and problem-solving communities would be better equipped to improve teaching and learning. In light of our experiences in cooperating to support students with disabilities, it was relatively easy for us at the O'Hearn to organize and implement these collaborative groups around the system's new guidelines.

One area in which all schools were asked to collaborate more was in looking at student work (LASW). Schools were supposed to form teams of teachers who would meet a few times each month to examine students' written work, to compare it to the grade-level standard, and to discuss strategies for improvements. Each time that a team of teachers from different grade levels and specialty areas met, they first identified the criteria or rubrics for excellent work or they came to consensus as to what excellence should be. Then they examined various samples of students' work and identified both the strengths and the growth areas according to the set standards. Next, and most importantly, they discussed instructional strategies that they could try to help the students improve. At the O'Hearn, this process of LASW always included the work of some students who had disabilities and some who did not. For students like Rayba, who had intellectual disabilities, the standards were modified to easier levels according to recommendations of the IEP teams. For other students, whose disabilities did not include cognitive delays, the state- and district-set grade-level standards applied, but accommodations to help those students achieve the same level of rigor achieved by nondisabled students were often necessary.

Another area in which all schools were asked to collaborate more was in peer observations, sometimes referred to as collaborative coaching and learning (CCL). Basically, teachers within each school were asked to visit and observe each other's classrooms. This was radical for most schools because previously teachers seldom had the opportunity to see their colleagues in action. At the O'Hearn, all teachers were already used to teaming with another teacher and to having therapists and paraprofessionals come into their rooms at different times to work with designated students. With CCL, peer observations expanded because teachers also took turns visiting classrooms of other colleagues and at other grade levels. They were asked to observe and focus on particular teaching and learning issues such as these:

- How were students explaining their thinking in response to specific questions?
- How were students checking for accuracy on their multiple-step math problems?
- How were students engaged throughout the period, even when the teacher was not working directly with them?

- How did the students with disabilities interact with those without disabilities?
- Did all the students seem to be adequately challenged and appropriately supported?

Visiting teachers were asked to jot down evidence on the particular focus question and were expected to observe students both with and without disabilities. Subsequently, the observations and other information were shared with the hosting teachers. At the O'Hearn, we always tried to provide an opportunity, albeit short, for the visiting and hosting teachers to meet and discuss both the observations and any suggestions. It was imperative to set a protocol to ensure that these conversations were constructive and not evaluative. Evaluations were the responsibility of the principal and did not occur during CCL times. Peer observation was meant to be a collegial way for teachers to be better informed and more supportive about improving the quality of instruction.

Overall, the O'Hearn staff collaborated constructively and enthusiastically. In fact, inclusion of the students could not have happened without inclusion among the adults. Successful cooperation was critical both for the provision of daily services and for ongoing professional development and problem solving.

During instruction, there were typically two primary ways that staff got together in the same classrooms to help all students learn and succeed. Either one teacher assumed the primary lead of the class while the other adults provided assistance to individuals, or the staff split the class into groups and divided themselves accordingly. Whichever way that the teaming occurred, it was critical that each staff member was well informed of the lessons' objectives and activities and that each adult was effectively utilized to maximize student progress.

Teachers and paraprofessionals (sometimes referred to as teacher assistants or aides) were the primary instructors in classrooms on a daily basis. Although general and special education teachers at the O'Hearn still had some different responsibilities, they each worked and interacted with the entire class. Many visitors commented that it was not always easy to distinguish which teacher had which certification. That, I believe is a sign of good staff inclusion. Most classrooms also had part-time assistance from paraprofessionals. These teacher aides were usually designated to provide support to a few children with more significant disabilities. However, we strongly encouraged teachers and paraprofessionals to prepare children and organize the learning activities so that all students could experience working independently or interacting with peers without there always being an adult hovering over them.

Many other staff collaborated with classroom teachers and paraprofessionals and made arrangements to provide support both in classrooms and around the school. For example:

- The O'Hearn's nurse connected with teachers to designate when it would be most appropriate to check on students with medical needs and to decide whether these children could be served in classrooms to maximize instructional time or whether they needed to go to her office.
- The occupational therapist scheduled her services with teachers so that she could also assist designated students sometime in their rooms when it was time for handwriting or art and other times in the cafeteria when it was time to practice eating more independently.

- Conferring with teachers, the speech pathologist planned when she would present a phonics lesson to the entire class and when she would help a small group of students practice oral skills.
- The school secretary utilized special protocols suggested by staff for communicating with nonverbal students for the times that they came into the office.
- The custodian responded to a teacher's request and agreed to allow a student with intellectual disabilities to push around a cart with him some afternoons as part of a positive-behavior reward option for motivating the student to complete his class work.
- Depending on students' needs and teacher requests, the physical therapist worked with students in a separate area with special therapy equipment, in classrooms, in the halls, on the playground, and en route to the busing area.
- Using specially designed prompts and other techniques, the lunch monitor supported teachers by helping a student with autism make the transition back from the cafeteria.
- The music specialist reinforced vocabulary selected by the fifth-grade social studies teacher by inserting the words into popular tunes that the students would sing in the auditorium.

All of these layers of support required extensive cooperation. The staff members needed to demonstrate much more flexibility regarding their specific roles. They needed to plan in advance who was going to do what. Occasionally, this meant that people had to transcend some of their personal feelings about working with particular colleagues and stay focused on what was best for the children. Student performance was paramount.

When staff had differences of opinion about the strategies or approaches proposed for children, we tried to base decisions on the anticipated impact on students' learning in the context of our inclusive school. Many times, we had to agree to try something out and then meet again to assess its effectiveness.

In terms of ongoing professional development and problem solving, there was no way that any one teacher could be completely knowledgeable about all the strategies necessary to support students with so many different disabilities and diverse needs. Our staff had to develop expertise in various areas and needed to share this knowledge and experience with many colleagues. As principal, I facilitated staff's participation in selected workshops and I scheduled regular times for staff to meet in small groups to discuss specific issues and appropriate instructional strategies. However, because this officially scheduled time was usually not sufficient, additional special meetings were called. For a few years, I was able to provide extra time and even a small stipend for teachers who had developed a special expertise so that they could directly support more colleagues. The vast majority of the sharing at the O'Hearn, though, occurred voluntarily. Direct conversations, phone calls, and e-mail messages frequently occurred during lunch, before and after regular school hours, and on weekends and holidays.

Relationships among O'Hearn staff were overall quite positive. During break times, naturally, the staff shared experiences about their own lives, but considerable conversation also focused on students and their progress. The O'Hearn developed into a strong professional learning community. The staff's commitment to collaboration and their flexibility and creativity in helping each other with the many challenges of teaching and learning were critical factors in the O'Hearn's success.

7

COLLABORATION WITH STUDENTS

THE STUDENT'S CHALLENGE

*"I don't use the urinals, because my mother told me to sit
on the toilet every time that I pee."*

Levi was a bright and very verbal grade-two boy who was blind.
Although he was quite competent moving around using his
white cane, I noticed that he was frequently one of the last kids
in his class to enter the cafeteria for lunch after using the boys
bathroom. I asked him why he often took so long. He replied
that he usually had to wait until the toilet was available in order to pee. I asked him why he didn't use the urinals, and that's
when he informed me what his mother had directed him to do.

The reason that his mother had requested that he sit on the
toilet at home even when urinating was probably because boys
tend to spray a bit and because his mother did not want to
bother cleaning up the regular and perhaps his extra misplaced
urine. Up until the second grade, Levi had attended classes on
the other side of the building, and he had never used the urinals in that bathroom. However, now he was on the side with a

lot more bathroom traffic. The boys bathroom on this side had many more urinals than toilets, and using the urinal was definitely more efficient. I assured Levi that his mother was in charge of how he used the bathroom at home, but that he and the other "big boys" would help move things along more quickly in the "big kids" bathroom by using the urinals when just peeing.

Levi agreed to try the urinals. The next day, with the teacher's permission, he ventured off to the bathroom alongside his friend Oscar. Oscar had agreed to accompany Levi on his first urinal jaunt. Getting to the urinal and peeing in it presented no problem for Levi. Unfortunately, though (as he had been accustomed to do when sitting on the toilet), Levi dropped his pants all the way to the floor. Even though this did not bother Levi, Oscar was mortified that his friend was so exposed. Oscar immediately finished off what he was doing and positioned himself directly behind his friend so that no one else could see the boy's behind. Once Levi had pulled up his pants and walked over to the sink to wash his hands, Oscar quickly informed Levi on the appropriate procedures for urination.

Subsequently, they headed back to their grade-two classroom. After sharing their saga in great detail with the teacher, they resumed their reading assignment. Each student took turns reading alternate pages from their copies of the same book. Levi was a very fluent reader, but Oscar sometimes had difficulty deciphering the more complex words. Using his fingers, Levi would quickly locate that difficult word on his Braille copy of the book and then he would help his buddy sound them out.

Unfortunately, not all student interactions at the O'Hearn were as positive as those between Levi and Oscar. There were always some students who were more annoying to, or more annoyed by, others. Some students carried grudges too long, and some even engaged in fights. We dealt with each specific situation according to various criteria, including its severity, its frequency, and the student's willingness to show remorse and make amends. In addition to intervening with individual situations, we also implemented a number of school-wide programs promoting conflict resolution and peaceful learning communities.

Overall, though, student interactions and behaviors at the O'Hearn were quite positive. Suspensions were rare, and office referrals were manageable. We witnessed how including students with disabilities engendered more caring and support. Even some of the students considered to have more problematic behaviors seemed calmer and less agitated, particularly when they had opportunities to be helpful with their classmates and to contribute. One of my most memorable moments as principal was at a graduation ceremony, when I listened to a speech given by a student who had been transferred to our school because of discipline problems. Although no one would ever claim that he had converted into an angel, his testimony about the impact of learning alongside a classmate who had extremely brittle bones brought many to tears.

There was no greater joy for me as principal than to witness the many ways that the students so naturally and spontaneously helped each other. Every student at the O'Hearn, whether the child had a disability or not, was expected sometimes to offer help and sometimes to receive it. Although students often had to complete their work and take care of things by themselves, in plenty of other times and in other ways, they were supposed to collaborate both in their classrooms and throughout the entire school.

As for Levi, in addition to his regular teachers, he received support from both a Braille instructor and a mobility specialist. He practiced these blindness skills in school and at home, and he became increasingly competent and independent. Levi continued to excel in all classes and scored at the advanced or proficient levels on standardized assessments. He was a popular student who interacted positively with most everyone. As a peer tutor (see below), he volunteered to read stories to kindergarteners through the use of books with Braille and print.

When he was in the middle of grade four, Levi's family moved to another town north of Boston. His new teachers visited our school before the transfer, and the O'Hearn staff collaborated with them during the transition. Levi made new friends quickly and continued to perform at advanced levels. When he entered his local high school, he joined the debating club and the wrestling team, and he was elected by his peers to be on the student council.

THE PRINCIPAL'S CHALLENGE

I needed students to help me on a daily basis with the overall functioning of the school, but most of this assistance had nothing to do with my blindness. For example, when the secretary took her lunch break each day, I recruited older students who were eating lunch at the same time to cover the office. The two students on office duty that day would be responsible for answering the phone, opening the front door, delivering messages or packages, putting some mail in staff boxes, and cleaning up around the offices. They could handle most of these tasks on their own, but sometimes they had to get me or another adult for clarification or to deal with a visitor whom they did not know. Other students helped me during breaks or before or after class time by distributing water bottles and cups, by setting up chairs in the auditorium, and by escorting younger children to different areas of the school. I too had to get involved to varying degrees with all these daily tasks, but the many areas of support provided by students certainly contributed tremendously to these efforts.

Students also supported me in other ways that did relate to my blindness. For example:

- I regularly asked students to read out loud what they had written.
- I frequently asked students to read out loud to me other print material that was not of a confidential nature.
- I occasionally asked students to help me navigate through crowded or congested areas.
- I sometimes asked students to help me locate items.
- I often asked students to describe artwork.
- Once in a while, I requested that students help me identify bus numbers.
- Sometimes, I requested that students describe the conditions of specific areas.

Most of these interactions were mutually rewarding and provided extra opportunities to connect. I certainly benefited by receiving specific types of support, and students benefited from the positive feelings from being helpful. Whether the support was related to my blindness or not, the students who assisted me definitely talked more with me as a result of all these moments together, and I gained valuable insights from these conversations about their lives and learning experiences.

Like other principals, I needed to check in regularly with students who frequently got themselves into various kinds of trouble. These were the kids who typically would fool around too much or who would sometimes say or do things that bothered other students or staff. I quickly learned that if I asked these students to assist me with particular tasks, then there was a better chance of preventing wrongdoings and redirecting them to something more positive. Admittedly, I would have had to connect more with these kids even if my vision had been normal, but perhaps I did use my blindness a bit more than necessary to solicit some of their extra energies and to help keep them on track.

The bottom line, though, was that we needed our students to help. Including children with significant disabilities, having an early-childhood program, and managing the tasks common to any elementary school required lots of support. There were indeed many times when members of the staff were not available to respond to immediate needs and the helping hands of children were usually welcome. Student collaboration at the O'Hearn was part of our culture; it was necessary, and it proved invaluable.

IMPLICATIONS FOR THE SCHOOL

Inclusion created additional opportunities for O'Hearn students to practice being helpful. Early on, though, we determined that all students, including those who had disabilities, needed to partake in that experience and joy. Below are descriptions of how O'Hearn students supported the school and others as peer tutors, morning helpers, and classroom helpers.

Peer Tutoring

Staff and parent representatives on the O'Hearn School Site Council strongly endorsed a peer tutoring program. This program provided students with structured opportunities to contribute to their school and to experience the value of community service. Grade three through five students were encouraged to volunteer to be a helper one day a week during their forty-minute lunch and recess periods. Students ate their lunch quickly either in the cafeteria or in the location of their peer tutoring job, and then they were expected to complete a variety of predetermined tasks. Almost all (over 90 percent) of the students in these grades volunteered to sacrifice one recess per week and stuck with their peer tutor assignments regularly throughout the school year. What was most unusual about the school's peer tutoring program was that students with disabilities were also expected to volunteer as helpers. In many other schools with peer tutoring programs, students with disabilities were often only expected to be the recipients of help. We were adamant that all students, including those with significant needs, should experience the responsibility and the opportunity of contributing.

In addition to her regular classes, a teacher provided excellent coordination of the peer tutoring program. With input from other staff, she assigned each student a particular job at a specific time each week. Many staff collaborated with her to make the experience worthwhile both for the peer tutor and for the person or area receiving the help. Students received varying degrees of guidance on keeping to their schedule and adequately fulfilling their tasks. Some extra planning and support were clearly necessary for some of the students with disabilities.

Peer tutoring jobs that students with disabilities completed once a week during their forty-minute lunch and recess period included the following:

- A girl with autism came to the office with a nondisabled peer and greeted each person who entered the front door by saying, "Welcome to the O'Hearn."
- A boy with Down syndrome assisted the art teacher in another class by passing out and collecting materials and helping with the cleanup.
- A student with physical disabilities supported younger children in their language arts class by checking their writing journals and by making suggestions for improvements.
- A student with learning disabilities assisted younger students working on computers with various software programs.
- A boy with emotional problems was an energetic and popular helper in an early-childhood class.
- A student with autism, along with a classmate, went to classrooms to empty the recycle boxes into a large rolling barrel.
- With the support of an occupational therapist, students with intellectual disabilities distributed requested materials (pencils, paper, crayons, etc.) to teachers in classes around the school.
- Along with two classmates, a student with multiple disabilities accompanied and helped kindergarten children during their lunch and recess.

Students without disabilities certainly provided these same services described above and many other important services for children and for the school as a whole, and their support was extremely valuable. However, it was unusual—or at least impressive—for many adults to witness students with disabilities also serving as helpers. Many adults presumed that the disabled children would be the recipients of help and not the providers. Interestingly, though, from the perspective of O'Hearn students, who were used to inclusion, peer tutoring was considered a regular school activity that should be expected of everyone, whether the student had a disability or not.

Some peer tutors with and without disabilities needed and received extra coaching to help them do their jobs better. Much of this guidance was in the areas of appropriate interactions and collaboration with other students and adults. The school benefited greatly from the many services provided by peer tutors. At the end of every school year, we celebrated their contributions at a peer-tutoring award ceremony. The students appreciated their certificates and relished the special party and extra attention. Equally important, peer tutors felt much satisfaction and learned a great deal from the experiences of making a difference for others.

Morning Helpers

We needed help at arrival time. Every morning, a different class of older students was assigned to be morning helpers for that particular day of the week. Morning helpers welcomed and stayed next to young children or next to students who had complex challenges and who benefited from assistance while they were waiting outside until the morning bell rang. If the weather was cold, the children waited inside the building in the back corridor. When the bell rang, morning helpers escorted their designated buddies to either the breakfast area or their classrooms.

As with peer tutoring, the expectations were that all grade three through five students should be morning helpers. Staff developed creative ways for some of the older students who had disabilities to contribute as morning helpers. For example:

- A boy who operated his own wheelchair rolled alongside and talked with a young student, who held on to the handle of the wheelchair until they arrived at the kindergarten classroom.
- A girl who needed help maneuvering her own wheelchair carried the backpack of a young child on her lap.
- A student with intellectual disabilities held the log-in clipboard for the staff member who was marking the arrival time of buses.
- A boy with emotional disorders stood by the door and asked students to walk quietly and keep to the right.
- A girl with autism carried a letter from a parent to the office.
- A boy with autism counted the numbers of students who came off the buses.

As with peer tutoring, all of these tasks were also completed by students without disabilities. This support occurred only during the fifteen minutes before classes began and only once a week, so they did not interfere with learning. Morning helpers provided an important service to the school, and many of them started their school day with a sense of contributing and accomplishment.

Classroom Helpers

In addition to peer tutoring and morning helpers, there were many other ways that children could be helpful to the school community. Teachers in every classroom identified tasks that students could do to help others and to contribute to the class as a whole. These classroom jobs were usually coveted by the children and were rotated so that all had opportunities to participate. Perhaps what was most impressive of all, though, was the many informal ways that children naturally helped each other throughout the school day. Visitors to the school always commented on this, and we all felt very proud that this was so obviously a part of the school culture. Kindness is an important virtue, and we gave our students plenty of opportunities to practice it.

Sometimes, of course, some students volunteered to help so that they could avoid their own schoolwork. Except for the peer tutoring and morning helper responsibilities, which we treated like jobs, students were usually not given permission to stop what they were doing and go help someone else unless they had first made a strong effort to finish their assignments set by their teachers. Opportunities to be helpful actually served to motivate some students to complete their class work more quickly. Developing a sense of being a contributor also helped some reduce problematic behaviors.

This spirit of student collaboration was clearly evident at the O'Hearn. To varying degrees, everyone needed and benefited from some help, and everyone was supposed to help and benefited from being helpful. Collaboration was promoted and practiced on a regular basis and not just during the designated times. All students were encouraged and praised for their efforts to be supportive with both children and adults. Including students with disabilities had certainly stretched the parameters of student-to-student collaboration, and the O'Hearn community was definitely more compassionate and more responsive as a result of this inclusion.

8

※

COLLABORATION WITH FAMILIES

THE PARENT'S CHALLENGE

"Please help me try to get Brittany to walk."

This was the plea of a mother of a grade four student who had cerebral palsy and moderate intellectual disabilities. Brittany was a very cheerful student who was popular with peers. She enjoyed participating in most class and school-wide activities, but she needed a great deal of support and curriculum modification. Her parents were pleased with Brittany's overall progress and were delighted with how she used a device with prerecorded responses for communication and a software program with pictures and symbols for reading and writing. Brittany and her family lived on the first floor of a triple-decker house that had a ramp by the back door. Given Brittany's age and increasing size, though, her mother was anxious about getting her walking and moving more independently. It was becoming increasingly difficult to travel around the community with her and particularly to carry her upstairs and downstairs into relatives' and friends' houses.

Because of her physical and cognitive impairments, Brittany's pediatrician thought it unlikely that she was going to walk. Likewise, the school's physical therapist, who had provided services to Brittany for five years, did not think that walking was possible. Brittany's mother hoped that it could happen and pledged to reinforce the recommended techniques on a daily basis. She was a family leader who encouraged other families to involve children with disabilities as much as possible in their communities, and now she was advocating for her own daughter.

Even though we had doubts about Brittany's ability to walk, the staff agreed to collaborate with the parents to make a concerted effort over the following three months to try to help Brittany learn to walk. Several strategies were employed in this effort:

- The physical therapist increased her direct services with Brittany and provided weekly consultation with staff and family on appropriate walking techniques.
- The teachers made arrangements twice a day for Brittany to transfer from her wheelchair and to stand in class using the prone stander.
- A paraprofessional stood behind her and held her upright to practice supported walks a few times each day.
- When it was time to go to the cafeteria for lunch (one of Brittany's favorite times of the day), a selected student walked backward in front of her and encouraged her (she was still supported by an adult) to move along.
- Brittany's family practiced supported walking with her every day in the apartment and around the neighborhood.

Unfortunately, despite a few months of intensive efforts and despite excellent collaboration between Brittany's family and the staff, she still did not demonstrate any improvements in her capacity to walk. Her parents accepted that walking was probably not going to happen for her. The family considered an electric wheelchair, but, for a variety of reasons—including her safety and the weight of the proposed chair—elected to keep the manual one. Brittany continued to move around in her wheelchair at school, sometimes pushing it herself for short distances, but mostly helped along by classmates or staff.

For grade six, her parents sent her to the nearby middle school, which was designated as the inclusive pathway for O'Hearn students. Brittany continued to make slow but steady improvements in her abilities to communicate, read, and write using assistive technology. She also continued to be a popular student and enjoyed most of her teachers and classes. Her mother participated on that school's parent council and joined a citywide committee to plan for more inclusive options in the district.

Although Brittany did not walk, other children at the O'Hearn did develop the capacity to walk despite their doctors' predictions that they would be unlikely to do so. There were also other students like Brittany who never walked independently, but who did make significant progress in other developmental and academic areas. Frankly, we did not know the possibilities for students with disabilities until we tried appropriate interventions and support. In all cases, communication and collaboration with parents were critical factors for students' development and success.

THE PRINCIPAL'S CHALLENGE

Walking around the school with a white cane while escorting parents to a particular location was not a challenge for me, except that I often had to slow down for them, because they did not move as quickly as I did. In other ways, though, O'Hearn parents supported me in ways related to my blindness:

- Because I was not always so adept at recognizing their voices as I was with most of their children, parents whom I encountered around the school or in the neighborhood were gracious about greeting me and identifying themselves by name.
- Parents usually read doctor notes or other written documents for the school out loud for me.
- Sometimes I enlisted parents to help me locate items such as instructional materials, misplaced brooms, or the homemade brownies.
- Occasionally, parents gave me a ride home after an evening or community meeting.

Most of my interactions with parents, though, had little to do with my eyesight or lack thereof. Having firsthand experience of the complexities of parenting, I recognized the responsibilities and efforts that O'Hearn families had in raising their own children. Parenting is hard work. It can be rewarding, but it can also be frustrating. Raising children with disabilities posed some additional challenges. I respected the many ways that O'Hearn families supported their own children's learning and was grateful for their caring about all children and working to better the school as a whole.

I genuinely enjoyed talking with O'Hearn parents and guardians about their children and their progress. Many of these adults would also share stories about situations at home. Over the years, I got to know many families quite well. There were, of course, times when parents voiced particular questions or concerns regarding their child and the school. Usually, these involved issues such as grades, assignments, schedules, routines, or interactions with other students or staff. Unless there were an emergency or a concern over safety, parents were supposed to communicate with their children's teachers first. When family members needed to meet with me, I would try to demonstrate active listening by acknowledging the parents' specific concerns as I heard them. Sometimes I was able to offer an immediate response, but at other times, I needed to investigate further. Occasionally, additional meetings with me or other staff were warranted. Unless there were unusual circumstances, most issues were resolved quickly, and I based decisions on what I believed was best for the child according to school policies or other general principles of fairness.

Parents of students who had disabilities had additional opportunities to discuss their children's needs and special services at IEP meetings. If the meeting participants could not agree on specific issues, the team sometimes designated a time to reconvene with additional information. Parents as well as school staff sometimes contacted special education administrators at the central office for clarification on specific issues. Federal law also guaranteed due-process rights for parents if they were not satisfied with IEP recommendations or implementation, and a parent could request mediation or possible hearings for further resolution.

I remember working with two families whose boys used wheelchairs and had multiple disabilities. Unfortunately, both boys were involved in accidents in our school courtyard during the same month. The first boy had been hit in the face by a soccer ball that a classmate had kicked and that his buddy for the day had been unable to stop. The boy was initially quite upset and had a slight bruise on his face, but it seemed—and the school nurse confirmed this—that he was otherwise fine. The second boy scraped his face and arm more seriously on the asphalt when his wheelchair, which a classmate was pushing quickly, had flipped over after hitting a bump. He was a little more banged up and needed to see a doctor to get some stitches. Both of these boys were sturdy and were going to be fine.

The outcomes of these incidents typified the difference in family responses. Interestingly, the grandmother and guardian of the first boy insisted that he never go outside again when the others were playing with balls and that he be assigned his own paraprofessional. The mother of the second boy who had been injured spent as much time expressing concern for the classmate who had been pushing her son. She did not want him to feel bad and acknowledged that it was normal for nine-year-olds to get some scrapes once in a while. With both children, we took immediate precautions to minimize further accidents. However, it was not surprising that the grandmother of the first boy requested an IEP meeting, and we reluctantly yielded to her request that her grandson be transferred to a small, substantially separate classroom in another school. The second boy continued playing outside with his friends and was happily included.

Some of my conversations with parents were difficult. It was understandable that parents would get emotional about some of the issues affecting their children and about the urgency they felt. I tried to listen, to be supportive, and to keep things calm. Most of the time, the issues were resolved satisfactorily. Sometimes, we had to agree to disagree. On rare occasions, if parents became overly agitated, I reminded everyone that we were in a school and needed to be civil or else the meeting would end. I also offered parents the names and contact information of my supervisor or other officials if the parents were not satisfied with my recommendations.

Blindness was not an impediment during stressful conversations with parents. Compassion, wisdom, and conviction were qualities far more important than sight. If anything, my being blind might have diffused some tense situations. Using my white cane to maneuver to the cooler to offer agitated parents some water probably helped dismiss any images of me being the stereotypical mean ogre of a principal. Kindness and sensitivity were always important.

I remember one grandmother who usually came to my office to vent every few months. I admired her for having assumed guardianship for two rambunctious boys whose mother (her daughter) had been incarcerated. Unfortunately, she was a bit overprotective and frequently cajoled the boys to name anyone who might be bothering them. During her emotional meetings with me, she often handed me a list with names of other children and even sometimes staff who were identified by her grandsons as the ones who had allegedly picked on them over the preceding weeks. After listening to part of her life story for a while, I would hand the list back to her and ask her to read the names on the list out loud so that I could log them on to my Braille note taker or my talking computer. Remembering that I was blind, she would often say something like, "Honey, don't you worry about this. You are doing a great job." I'd usually responded by telling her that we would keep "our eyes" on the boys in school and that they were blessed to have her as their grandmother.

I'll never forget participating in a national conference focusing on special education and parents' rights. A federal official who was a keynote speaker suggested that parents needed to get "mean" to get what their children needed. I raised my hand and publicly disagreed with the official, explaining that being assertive and being mean are very different. Advocating for one's child in ways that are civil is admirable. Behaving in ways that offensive or disruptive should not be condoned.

Unfortunately, over the years, I witnessed a few rare situations where some adults did act mean by resorting to name calling, screaming, and even threatening harm. Usually this occurred because of a disagreement over the way that we provided services, graded a student, or handled discipline. These behaviors have no place in schools and require appropriate and quick responses to ensure the safety of children and staff and the smooth functioning of the school. When confronted with such situations, I asked the individuals to immediately stop the inappropriate behaviors or to leave the school premises. A few times, I actually had to physically block some individuals from proceeding to areas of the school, because I had reason to believe that they would be harmful to students or staff or very disruptive to teaching and learning. Sometimes, we needed to call for police support, and sometimes, according to School Department guidelines, we initiated further legal actions.

These volatile situations were not the norm, but all principals, whether they are sighted or not, need to be prepared to deal with them. Fortunately, the vast majority of the interactions with parents at the O'Hearn were extremely cordial, and most other interactions were at least civil. Even when there were disagreements, the staff and I acknowledged that parents almost always advocated for what they believed was in the best interests of their children.

IMPLICATIONS FOR THE SCHOOL

Parent collaboration would emerge as one of the O'Hearn's hallmarks. Interestingly, before inclusive education started in 1989, the previous staff had identified the lack of family involvement as the major growth area for the school. Involving parents of students with disabilities would change that. Many of our families already advocated extensively for their children to be included, and they expected to continue to be actively involved in their son's and daughter's new school. We committed to being welcoming to all families, to be respectful of their responsibilities and roles as their children's primary educators, and to collaborate with families to help them be more knowledgeable about and supportive of their children's learning.

Family Outreach

In our first year of inclusive education, a small committee was formed with parent and teacher leaders to identify ways of increasing parent involvement at the O'Hearn. The group decided that major outreach to families was necessary to demonstrate how the culture of the school could change and be more welcoming for everyone. Many group members stressed how families who had children with disabilities also needed to be included in this effort.

The committee wrote a proposal to solicit funds for promoting family involvement and submitted the proposal to the Institute for Responsive Education, which, in 1989, was an organization associated with Boston University. The institute approved our proposal and provided resources for child care and light food at parent meetings and for hiring a part-time family outreach coordinator. This dedicated coordinator, who eventually became an O'Hearn parent herself, lived in a nearby Dorchester neighborhood. She helped recruit a group of twenty parent outreach volunteers. The volunteers represented the ethnic and linguistic diversity of the school, and some of them had children with disabilities and thus were strong advocates for these students. In preparation for the outreach, the volunteers agreed to participate in monthly evening training sessions and other meetings focusing on strategies to improve overall family involvement.

These family outreach training and meeting sessions were helpful in providing opportunities for the volunteers to share both the joys and the challenges of being parents. The volunteers, who were very articulate about the complexities of raising children, shared and agreed upon specific ways for approaching other parents and encouraging their participation in the school. As part of the outreach initiative, the parent volunteers committed to visiting the homes of all families whose children were newly assigned to the O'Hearn. They also agreed to visit and try to connect with families whom the staff felt might benefit from additional support. Extra care was made to match families so that we could tap into the expertise of a parent who spoke another language or who had the experience of raising a child with a disability. Usually, two O'Hearn parent volunteers traveled together for the initial home visits. These outreach volunteers provided information about the O'Hearn such as concrete tips both for getting involved in school activities and for helping children with homework. They also provided a gift of some books recommended by teachers for the families to read at home with their children. Some volunteers established closer and ongoing relationships with a few families who needed and accepted additional support. Additionally, the volunteer parents offered suggestions and made some referrals to help the families address issues such as housing, food and nutrition, child rearing, and even addictions.

The impact of the O'Hearn Family Outreach Program was powerful. Many parents expressed how wonderful it was having other parents visit and welcome them to the school community. Most of the parents who were visited committed to participating in upcoming school events and to collaborating closely with teachers to help their children progress. Many acknowledged a deep appreciation for the parent-to-parent support that was offered. Teachers praised the efforts of the outreach volunteers and recognized the many ways that family involvement had been transformed as a result. Most importantly, all agreed that increased family involvement was an essential factor that contributed to students' academic success and other school-wide improvements.

The family outreach volunteers became key leaders at the O'Hearn. They proposed a number of initiatives that were discussed and approved by the parent and teacher representatives serving on the O'Hearn School Site Council (SSC). Some of these programs were implemented in the early 1990s and continued as strong components of the O'Hearn throughout the following years. All these initiatives had an impact on student achievement, and four of them are described below.

Home Reading Program

Helping students to read more and to read at higher levels became a major school-wide priority. In addition to needing to elevate the quality of reading instruction in school, we needed to increase the time that children were reading at home. A comparison of the school's top- and lower-performing readers had revealed a relatively dramatic difference in time that these groups of children spent reading or being read to at home. Therefore, the SSC decided to adopt home reading requirements. After much discussion with parents and listening to their concerns that some afternoons and evenings could be very hectic, the council determined that families should submit a home reading contract each week. The contract documented that the families' children had read or had someone reading with them at least four days per week for at least fifteen to thirty minutes, depending on the age of the child.

With the input of teachers, family outreach volunteers provided materials and worked directly with the families that struggled to fulfill this contract. Parents who did not speak English benefited from books either in their native language or in English with accompanying cassettes. Parents of children with print disabilities needed and appreciated adapted materials, including books with varying audio or tactile components. In subsequent years, digital or electronic books became increasingly popular and accessible. Additional books for O'Hearn families were acquired both through publicly funded programs like Reading Is Fundamental (RIF) and ReadBoston and through donations from individuals. Family leaders also helped circulate more books by organizing a book swap program whereby children could bring from their homes the books that they had finished reading and then trade them in at school for other books.

Home reading participation was monitored each week, and depending on the percentage of contracts submitted during each marking period, a grade was entered onto the students' report cards. Recognition and other incentives were given to the children who demonstrated that they were reading regularly at home most of the time. Teachers were responsible for notifying parents whose children either clearly fabricated what they had supposedly been reading or had not turned in any contracts. Subsequently, outreach volunteers were asked to connect with the families of the children who were still not fulfilling the home reading requirements. Although home reading participation had risen from a starting point of about 45 percent to slightly over 90 percent, some families were still not participating. Not surprisingly, a majority of the children from these families were also reading below grade level.

Interestingly, the family outreach volunteers organized a pizza party for these families. Some of the older students thought that it was a prank. Why would they be invited to an evening pizza party with their parents for neglecting to complete their home reading contracts? They were told that it would be a motivation party to help them start reading more. Through the persistence of the outreach volunteers and with the lure of pizza and a movie for the children while their parents were meeting, most of the identified families did attend the party. The discussion among parents while their children were in another room was moving. Parents and guardians shared with each other that they wanted their children to read more at home, but they felt overwhelmed with the daily struggles of parenting, including feeding, bathing, and cleaning for their children. A number of parents were doing this alone, either because they were single parents or because their spouses were working multiple jobs.

As parents themselves, the outreach volunteers were able to share some of their own struggles along with some of the strategies and routines that they had implemented in their own homes with their children. This contact and other continued support led to some improvements in home reading participation. The parents who had been contacted expressed appreciation for the support and felt more connected to the school, because of this connection to other parents.

As mentioned, the overall reading performance of students at the O'Hearn rose from the low average to the high average levels over the four years that inclusive education was phased in through grade five. Everyone believed that reading more at home was a contributing factor. The participation of students both with and without disabilities was important. Parents of children who had significant cognitive delays also read and shared stories with their children, and the other students noticed how the students with disabilities also had to submit reading contracts each week. Everyone was involved with home reading, and the leadership of family outreach volunteers was critical for the development of this successful program.

After-School Program

When inclusion started at the O'Hearn in 1989, all students went home after the regular six-hour school day. Some of the students were able to participate in sports, recreational, or cultural activities that were offered after school hours in the surrounding neighborhoods. Unfortunately, as was confirmed by the outreach volunteers who were conducting home visits, there were fewer of these opportunities for children with disabilities. Many of these programs did not accept or welcome certain students, particularly those with significant challenges. Outreach volunteers recommended that the O'Hearn consider providing inclusive opportunities for students after the regular school day. The SSC was very eager for this to occur, but we clearly needed additional resources. Family leaders collaborated with school staff to write a proposal to a state organization that was then called the Massachusetts Department of Mental Retardation. With that initial funding and by establishing a very reasonable sliding fee scale, the O'Hearn after-school program was launched in the early 1990s.

Over the years, many activities were offered through this after-school program, including math enrichment, challenger reading groups, assistive technology, woodworking, crafts, yoga, Shakespeare club, Irish step dancing, African drums and dancing, keyboard instruction, Spanish, cooking, inclusive Special Olympics, test preparation, homework help, and recreation. These programs were led by parents, by O'Hearn school staff, and by talented persons from the community or associated with various agencies. After-school activities were inclusive, and resources for a nurse and additional support staff were provided.

Parent leaders assumed the primary responsibility for coordinating and directing the O'Hearn after-school program. They worked closely with families and O'Hearn staff to ensure that the experiences were rewarding and fun. To keep the fees low and to offer scholarships, parent leaders wrote grants and coordinated many fund-raising activities. Some of these fundraisers, such as yard sales that stretched along the main street in front of the school, jazz nights with dinner and live entertainment, and talent shows with food and lots of family participation, also served as community-building experiences.

The after-school program proved to be a critical extension of the regular school day. Keeping the building open for an additional two hours with appropriate supervision also allowed O'Hearn teachers to stay late and offer tutoring and other services that otherwise could not had been provided. Many children attended the after-school program every day, and most others took advantage of at least some of the activities offered.

The O'Hearn after-school program received outside recognition as well. The leaders of the program were acknowledged by state and nonprofit groups for the excellence of the inclusive activities. A popular video documentary highlighting the program was produced with funds from the Federation for Children with Special Needs. Most importantly, children with and without disabilities enjoyed the many different activities and opportunities to socialize, and their learning continued to develop.

Parent-Teacher Conferences

Before inclusion was initiated at the O'Hearn, participation at parent-teacher conferences had historically been low. Previously, parent-teacher meetings involved the parents' standing in line and having a fairly rushed conversation around the report card. Parent and teacher leaders requested that this traditional format be changed. They proposed scheduling conferences in advance and allotting at least fifteen minutes per family, with opportunities for looking at student work, comparing it with the standards, and discussing strengths and growth areas. The leaders also wanted the teachers to suggest specific strategies and materials that families could use at home to accelerate student progress. This new parent-teacher conference format was endorsed by the SSC. As a result, homeroom teachers could only meet with eight families during the typical two-hour evening open house. Extra times were identified both during and after regular school hours to accommodate all the families for the expanded conferences.

In addition to the traditional notices inviting parents to the schedule conferences, outreach volunteers helped make phone calls and even arranged for rides if necessary to facilitate parents' attendance. If parents had seldom participated in a conference before, the teachers dedicated some extra time showing them more of their children's work and routines. We always strived to highlight the positives as well as some growth areas. Families were very pleased with the new format. They were more informed about their children's progress and about ways that they could further support their children's learning at home.

Curriculum Exhibitions

Parent leaders expressed that they were eager to learn more about the curricula and the rigorous new standards. The school had offered some informational workshops for families during the day and at night, but attendance was relatively modest, with anywhere between fifteen and thirty parents attending. Many parents voiced particular frustration with the new mathematics program. It was based on a constructivist approach quite different from the traditional way that most parents and teachers had learned math. Rather than the typical lecture-style presentation, outreach volunteers and teacher leaders proposed sponsoring a math night where children and parents could engage in some of the same activities and games that students experienced in the curriculum.

Because it was billed as a fun and interactive evening for the family, and because outreach volunteers helped encourage everyone to participate, close to two hundred children and adults attended the first math night. Families went from classroom to classroom, where teachers offered a range of interactive and fun math activities and games. Efforts were made to ensure that all children—those who were advanced and those who worked well below grade level—had meaningful ways to participate. Most participants enjoyed this experience tremendously, and the parents gained a better understanding of the new math curriculum.

As a result of the success of that first math night and others, parents requested additional opportunities to learn more about other curricula. It seemed, though, that attendance was higher when the children were involved rather than when professionals were the only ones presenting. Teacher and parent leaders on the SSC agreed to promote classroom exhibitions, where parents could observe their children demonstrating some aspect of the curricula in action. Over the years, classroom exhibitions covered a range of themes, including poetry, biographies, science experiments, Caribbean festivals, computer programs, testimonials to mothers and other women important to children, country reports, and specific techniques for solving complex and multiple-step math problems. All the children in the class participated in the exhibitions and had something to share. Some students with significant disabilities required a little more support from peers or staff, but everyone recognized their efforts and accomplishments.

Attendance at all classroom exhibitions was high. Almost every student had one or more family members who participated. Teachers worked hard organizing the students' presentations. Parent volunteers helped by making phone calls to other parents and organizing refreshments. If a parent could not attend because of work or illness, he or she was encouraged to send another relative or family friend. The treats that were provided were always a big hit. Most importantly, the parents were delighted to see the children sharing and demonstrating their work and knowledge, and the adults gained a better appreciation for the various curricula and for overall student performance.

Additional Family Involvement

Although the four programs described above and initiated by the family outreach volunteers did continue at the O'Hearn, the formal family outreach program and home visits ceased in the early 2000s. Basically, because we were unable to fund a part-time organizer, the coordination of the group could not be sustained. Family leaders were still active on the SSC, and all parents and guardians were automatically members of the O'Hearn School Parent Council.

Over the years, the parent council supported the school and families in a number of ways. For about ten years, it coordinated a family center, where, once a week, parents could come during the day to a designated room in the school, meet other parents, and share some light refreshments. Sometimes there was a designated topic for discussion such as ideas for nutritious snacks or holiday gifts, and sometimes there was nothing scheduled and the meeting was just social. The council also sponsored several day and evening workshops for parents. With assistance from the Federation for Children with Special Needs, many O'Hearn parents who had children with disabilities received valuable training and information about rights and services. Other meetings sponsored by the council focused on a range of topics, including school uniforms, fund-raising, technology, inclusive pathways and other options, curricula and assessments, partnerships with agencies and organizations, and playgrounds. The council also planned teacher-appreciation lunches and International Night family dinners.

In addition to all these efforts, many individual parents contributed greatly to particular classrooms and to the school as a whole. Here are some of the ways they helped:

- Donated books, rugs, paper tissues, and other items on teachers' wish lists
- Accompanied classes on field trips
- Help set up classrooms and built shelves and storage bins
- Read books to classes and shared stories of their travels and work
- Served as classroom leaders, fostering communication with families and helping coordinate special events
- Wrote articles for the school newsletters
- Lobbied at meetings and with city leaders on behalf of the school
- Assisted with major cleanups
- Acquired resources, including food and educational materials, and arranged for special presenters, from the community

It was hard for newer staff to imagine that family involvement at the O'Hearn had once been a major weakness. Overall, parents' support for the school was tremendous, and their involvement in their own children's learning was very valuable. O'Hearn parents, both those whose children had disabilities and those whose children were typical, became strong advocates for inclusion. They presented at conferences and workshops and shared how inclusive education had benefited their children. Parents proved to be critical partners to the O'Hearn's overall success.

I remember overhearing some parents at the beginning of one school year. They were talking outside the main doors while waiting for their children at dismissal time. When one parent of a new student was asked how things were going for her daughter, she replied that there seemed to be no problems but she was concerned because her child was in a class with a lot of "retarded" children. Immediately, three other parents politely but assertively explained to her how they had decided to send their children to the O'Hearn precisely because it was inclusive. They further elaborated on how having kids with cognitive delays and special needs along with the collaborative teaching and diversified instruction also created many opportunities for their sons and daughters. Their quick and articulate responses, along with the involvement of so many parents in programs and endeavors described above, typified the power of collaboration with families at the O'Hearn.

9

·:◈:·

COLLABORATION WITH OUTSIDE SUPPORTERS

THE VISITOR'S CHALLENGE

"Would you mind if we came by with some visitors?
There should be about fifty of us."

This was the request made in the early 1990s by an official from the Boston Foundation, which is one of the largest charitable organizations in New England. The official wanted to show some of the foundation's leading donors what inclusion looked like. Even though we at the O'Hearn were still in our initial years of implementation, the official wanted to visit the school. Although we had never hosted such a large group at one time, we felt that we should accommodate them. The Boston Foundation coordinated contributions to many schools in Boston, and the O'Hearn had recently been awarded the coveted Support for Early Education Development (SEED) grant, which is described below.

There's no easy way to take fifty people around a school, crowd them as a group into one classroom at a time, and expect that teaching and learning would continue normally. Therefore, after a brief overview, we divided everyone into groups of five and gave each group a different schedule. Then we sent the visitors off on their own unescorted tour for sixty minutes so that they all could visit a number of classrooms without bunching up.

According to the donors, what impressed them the most was how inclusion appeared to be so ordinary to the children. The adults were flabbergasted that students considered it no big deal to be sitting next to, and mingling with, children who used wheelchairs, who were reading and writing with special gadgets, who communicated through devices, or who needed specialized medical equipment. The visitors were amazed that teaching and learning seemed to continue and to be happening at fairly rigorous levels. That is exactly what we wanted to hear.

Over the years, the O'Hearn entertained many visitors. Most were parents or professionals from the Boston area, but many came from other states and even countries. Usually, we scheduled one or two visitation mornings per month and limited the total number of visitors on any given day to around fifteen individuals. We asked the visitors to arrive at a designated time. Often, they were greeted at the door by a few students with disabilities who benefited from practicing speech and communication. We gave the visitors a brief overview and orientation to the school. Then they were free to observe in any area of the school except for rooms where there was testing or confidential meetings.

Visitors were asked to follow general guidelines. They could observe teaching and learning throughout the school, but we preferred that there be no more than a total of five visitors present in any one classroom at a time. They were invited to enter the rooms and stand along the side or in the back, but they were not supposed to interrupt teaching and learning. Random picture taking was not allowed. At the discretion of the teachers, the visitors could sometimes talk briefly with the staff or even listen to a student share his or her work. This usually occurred when there was time before a transition or when students were working independently. We asked, however, that the visitors address most of their questions and comments to me or other available staff outside the classroom.

Over the years, a few interesting situations with visitors arose:

- A second-grade girl politely told a prominent visiting city official to move since he was blocking her view of the blackboard.
- A visitor who came from another country and spoke little English crouched in front of a student with obvious disabilities and gestured for the child to smile so that he could take pictures. We reminded the adult that photographs were not permitted.
- An educator who was trying to be helpful showed a student how to convert fractions to decimals using a procedure different from what the teacher had just taught.
- An administrator from another school system was asked to stop looking through the drawers of a teacher's desk.
- A mother who hoped to enroll her son at the O'Hearn the following year started relating the child's long medical history in detail to staff who were busy right then.

The teachers gently suggested that she meet with the school's nurse.

- A small group of visiting teachers started arguing noisily in a classroom about how inclusion might work in their district. They were encouraged to continue their conversation in the corridor.

These situations were relatively rare. Most visitors clearly recognized and respected that the school was in session and that teaching and learning were the priority. Because visitors were fairly common and because children were already used to different adults coming in and out of their rooms, O'Hearn students usually stayed on task during visitation times. People who visited the school generally expressed appreciation and shared many positive comments. We kept in contact with some of our visitors and encouraged O'Hearn staff to visit other schools and programs. Observing other teachers, particularly effective ones, is a powerful professional development tool. The O'Hearn staff and I had much to learn from each other, from other educators, and from outside supporters.

THE PRINCIPAL'S CHALLENGE

When inclusion started at the O'Hearn in 1989, the school had no money in its savings account; nor did it have any petty cash. Fortunately, there were plenty of basic materials like paper, pencils, pens, and crayons. We were also extremely grateful for the $5,000 allocated by the deputy superintendent to partner with VSA Massachusetts and to contract its teaching artists. Otherwise, there was no extra money for adaptive equipment, no funds for professional development, and nothing for special requests. A candy sale brought us some quick dollars, but was not sufficient for the long haul.

We needed to hustle. Blindness was no impediment for that. If anything, we probably got a little more attention when applying for grants since receiving requests from a blind principal whose school was including lots of kids with disabilities was somewhat of an anomaly.

My biggest challenge connecting with outside supporters was that I had so little time to do so. The daily work of a principal took most of my energy. Because teaching and learning were the priorities, I tried to spend a couple of hours each day in classrooms. The lunch periods and recesses also usually required some involvement. What's more, arrival and dismissal times at a school located on a busy city street with no parking lot demanded that I spend some time each morning and afternoon checking that staff were deployed and that things were going well. Every day always brought some additional surprises and problems to my attention.

Whenever someone from an outside agency requested that he or she come to the school and have a conversation with me, I usually accepted, but warned the person that more than ten minutes of uninterrupted time in my office was a luxury. Walking around the school and talking was sometimes the most realistic meeting format. If someone wanted to meet me around lunch, I encouraged the visitor to drop by and accompany me anytime during the three shifts of the students' forty-minute lunch periods. As principal, I was responsible for overseeing the cafeteria and outdoor recess for all children with support from lunch monitors and paraprofessionals while the teachers had their lunch breaks. This daily joy usually kept me on the move. Thus, the hectic schedule of a principal meant that most of my networking with outside supporters happened in brief spurts during the school day. After-school hours were best for in-depth communications and meetings. Most proposals and reports had to be written on weekends and during vacations.

Although visitors can ultimately benefit a school by providing financial or collaborative support, a principal's first duty is always to the students and staff. Therefore, it is imperative to stand firm about time commitments to visitors and to avoid falling into the trap of becoming strictly a public relations agent. Teaching and learning has to be the priority.

IMPLICATIONS FOR THE SCHOOL

The many layers of support that the O'Hearn started receiving in 1989 from businesses, nonprofits, community groups, universities, government agencies, and individual benefactors were extremely valuable. Neither the staff nor the students could have accomplished as much as they did without this generous support. One organization, VSA Massachusetts, has been partnering with the O'Hearn from 1989 to the present. Another group, the Jewish Literacy Coalition, continued providing volunteers to read one-on-one with O'Hearn students from the mid-1990s. Sustained support for schools is extremely valuable. Nevertheless, groups or individuals who contributed even one time were important to us. Although it is impossible to name and describe all those who assisted the O'Hearn over the years, we are most grateful for their contributions.

Three types of outside support exemplified the outstanding collaboration that the O'Hearn enjoyed in its mission of helping all children learn and succeed. As described in the following sections, we received invaluable assistance from the central offices of the Boston School Department; from businesses, as exemplified by the law firm of Goodwin, Procter, and Hoar; and from universities, such as the Harvard Graduate School of Education.

Institutional Support: Central Offices of the Boston School Department

Although the folks who worked at the central offices of the Boston School Department were not technically outside supporters, their day-to-day routines and responsibilities were quite different from those of the people who worked inside schools. Over my twenty years as principal, the O'Hearn received regular assistance from many persons working out of the central offices. I was also fortunate to have served under talented superintendents and deputy superintendents and to have worked in a city led by two outstanding mayors who were very committed to public education. All of these leaders, in their own ways, were supportive of the O'Hearn as an inclusive school and of me as a principal. Given their many responsibilities in a large district, their visits to the school were infrequent but noteworthy.

Fortunately, the school's overall academic standing was strong, the students' behavior was mostly positive, and staff and parent satisfaction was generally high, so we needed fewer interventions than some other schools did. However, whenever there was a serious issue or we needed some quick support or advice, the Boston school and city leaders were there for us. This did not mean that we always got what we requested, but they listened to our concerns and explained their decisions in the context of the system's policies.

Several key initiatives led by central office leaders at the Boston School Department had a tremendous impact on promoting inclusion at the O'Hearn. Chapter 6 highlighted some of our efforts to realize the mandate of developing professional learning communities. In particular, starting in the mid-1990s, the School Department provided training to promote both looking at student work (LASW) and collaborative coaching and learning (CCL). The school department offered professional development and prepared materials promoting LASW and CCL. It designated funds so that schools could hire part-time coaches who worked directly with teachers and principals to develop skills in these areas. This concerted effort at the O'Hearn mobilized us to bring staff together and to discuss what we as professionals could do to help students improve. The collective wisdom and the collaboration that this engendered assisted us in figuring out additional ways to benefit both students with disabilities and those without.

Another priority that central office personnel helped us learn and implement through training and coaching was the workshop approach. Although specific materials changed over the years, Boston teachers were expected to use the workshop format throughout the curricula. According to this approach, teachers were supposed to start lessons by condensing main points into five to ten minutes of direct teaching presented to the whole group. Next, a majority of the class time was spent with students engaged in activities such as reading, writing, computing, discussing topics, conducting experiments, integrating the arts, or making things. Students did this working either on their own or in small groups. This meant that teachers were lecturing less and spending more time checking on students' understanding and pointing out helpful strategies. Finally, at the end of the period, the whole group came back together and spent about five minutes for some selected sharing and for highlighting key points. The workshop model served as an excellent format for implementing inclusive education. In classrooms like the O'Hearn, there were always some students working way below grade level, most around grade level, and a few well above grade level. Because students spent most of their time working individually or in small groups, teachers and support staff had more opportunity to instruct students at their particular skill levels within the same topic areas that the rest of the class was involved in.

Increasing the use of technology was also identified in Boston as a system-wide goal. Many staff from the central office collaborated with us to figure out how we could better integrate technology throughout the school. Like many schools in Boston, the O'Hearn initially offered computer classes in our computer lab. The main problem with this was that all students, and particularly those with disabilities, needed to use technology more as an everyday learning tool and not just once or twice a week as a special class. With this in mind, we dismantled our computer lab in the late 1990s and moved most of the computers into the classrooms. Professionals from central office and city hall supported us with ongoing upgrades of the school's infrastructure for technology. They connected us to organizations like Kurzweil, the Center for Applied Technology (CAST), Intel, and Achieve 3000—groups with which we collaborated to acquire additional equipment and software. The central offered training, provided technical assistance for staff, and helped O'Hearn teachers identify and utilize appropriate assistive technology for students with disabilities.

I personally also received valuable assistance from many Boston School Department professionals who helped me with a myriad of tasks. The vast majority of these tasks involved responsibilities common to the work of any principal. But a few tasks were definitely trickier for me due to blindness, and I greatly appreciated the additional support.

Department colleagues helped me gain access to various important written materials. For example, a specialist from the Office of Instructional Technology provided invaluable ongoing assistance by determining which of the many programs utilized by administrators in Boston could be made accessible and then by teaching me how to access them with my screen reader. Other department colleagues, who coordinated professional development, helped me receive books and articles in accessible format.

Paperwork—the bane of most principals, both sighted and blind—was often made easier through the assistance of Boston School Department colleagues. Human resource specialists, for example, helped me maneuver through the paperwork to process new staff. Lawyers occasionally helped me identify the appropriate forms needed for difficult situations involving specific students, staff, or family members. Staff at the Special Education Department helped decipher and relate the key points from the complicated IEP forms of new students whom they were going to assign to the O'Hearn.

Additionally, student evaluations and budgeting were made smoother by department assistance. For example, staff from Research and Evaluation collaborated with me periodically to review and analyze student data. Budget directors reviewed the school budget orally with me and helped me prepare a less cumbersome summary to share with staff and parent leaders.

On a more practical level, I enjoyed much thoughtful consideration from many members of the department. Many colleagues offered me rides to meetings and helped orient me to different surroundings (e.g., helping me locate the meeting room or the men's room). I especially appreciated colleagues' assistance in finding any tasty treats that might have been set out for meetings.

Not everything with the Boston Public Schools was always so rosy. Functioning in a large system definitely posed some challenges. The following examples also probably occurred in many other districts and would have certainly frustrated me just as much if I had been fully sighted.

- Some buses were often late getting students to the O'Hearn or picking them up on time after school.
- Some administrative reports seemed redundant or needlessly complex.
- Occasionally we were not allowed to interview or hire candidates for definite openings until much later than anticipated.
- A few central office staff were slow to return phone calls or respond to e-mails.
- The heat at the O'Hearn did not always circulate evenly.
- Although they had agreed not to do so, some staff working at the distribution center sometimes tried to unload materials in the middle of student arrivals.
- During economic downturns, budget reductions were always difficult to resolve.

Overall, though, leaders and staff working for the Boston School Department and for the City of Boston provided tremendous support for the O'Hearn. They gave us the opportunity and the backing to develop an inclusive school. They provided many resources, recognized our efforts, and, most importantly, valued the accomplishments of our children.

In terms of promoting inclusive education, I believe that Boston's record during the years that I was principal was mixed and incomplete. Central office leaders approved and supported a number of schools—besides the O'Hearn—that were committed to inclusion. Some entire schools and some programs within schools proved to be excellent in their implementation of inclusive education with overall high student achievement and with widespread recognition. However, Boston did not have a systemic plan for inclusion, and far too many students with disabilities spent most of their education in substantially separate classrooms. In some areas of the city, more so at secondary levels, there were either insufficient or no options for inclusive education, especially for students with intellectual or developmental issues.

As for students graduating from the O'Hearn, in the mid-1990s, the School Department did designate a nearby middle school as an inclusive pathway where O'Hearn students with disabilities and other Boston school students with disabilities could be included. Some of our students chose to attend this school, and parents of children who had intellectual disabilities were generally pleased. However, the overall academic performance of that middle school and the one that eventually replaced it was relatively low. As a result, except for students with cognitive delays, many of our families chose not to send their children to the pathway school. Instead, they selected other district and charter schools, which had higher student achievement but which, for the most part, did not offer inclusion, particularly for students with significant disabilities.

For school year 2010–2011, the Boston School Department intervened and instituted major changes in a number of schools to turn around their performance. Because of low test scores, the middle school that served as the inclusive pathway for O'Hearn students was identified as a turnaround school. Many new staff were hired, and new programs were implemented. In addition, in 2011, Boston officials were gathering input from parents and educators in order to draft a comprehensive plan to expand inclusive options. Hopefully, this plan, along with the efforts to transform schools, will lead to more high-quality, inclusive schools across the city.

Business Support: The Goodwin, Procter & Hoar Example

Over the years, many businesses and agencies have contributed significantly to schools in Boston, and the O'Hearn certainly has received numerous sources of support. Through the generosity of these contributors, the O'Hearn has acquire many additional materials and services, including books, computers, software programs, a sound system and curtains for the auditorium, keyboards, playground equipment, rugs, science materials, bus transportation and admissions for field trips, art materials, classroom furniture, special presenters, after-school staff, consultants, child care for meetings, and food for special events. We are extremely grateful and have benefited greatly from these and many other contributions.

The first business that supported the O'Hearn was Goodwin, Procter & Hoar (GP&H), which was the largest law firm in the city of Boston. The firm subsequently changed its name to Goodwin and Procter and has offices in Boston and elsewhere around the world. When inclusion started at the O'Hearn in

1989, GP&H was offering one Boston public school per year a $50,000 SEED grant. The idea behind the SEED grant was to help a promising school start a new initiative by providing the school with seeds of financial support. The application was fairly long and required that teachers and parents buy into the initiative. We were excited about this opportunity and drafted a strong proposal. When we were chosen as one of three finalists, representatives from the law firm and from the Boston Foundation came for a site visit. They were impressed by our commitment and initial efforts to promote inclusion. That year, we were very fortunate to be selected as a recipient for the SEED grant.

To provide some context for the significance of this grant, the yearly budget for materials and discretionary funds for the O'Hearn in 1990 was a total of approximately $12,000. This allocation covered photocopying costs, paper, books, and all other instructional materials. Receiving $50,000 was like winning the jackpot. The primary goal of the SEED grant was to help us foster cooperative learning and collaborative teaching in our inclusive classrooms. Funds were utilized to provide special workshops, hire consultants, offer stipends to staff for extra planning, purchase books and enrichment materials, pay for student field trips, pay for substitutes so that the staff could visit other schools, cover the costs of child care and food at parent workshops and meetings, and develop a school brochure and materials about inclusion.

The SEED grant proved to be extremely beneficial. Teachers felt validated spending extra time learning how to collaborate with their colleagues to plan and implement inclusion. Students thrived with the additional materials, enjoyed participating in team-building experiences with their peers, and were more engaged in their classes. Parents became more involved both with the school and with activities that supported their children's learning at home. As suggested in its name, the SEED grant did indeed help us "grow" inclusion more successfully at the O'Hearn.

In addition to these funds, we took advantage of the law firm's offer to develop a closer partnership with it. Approximately seventy O'Hearn students started a pen-pal relationship with seventy members of the law firm. Over the course of the year, each pen pal wrote and received approximately four letters. We decided that all letters should be sent together so that no student would ever feel left out. Some of the law firm members were able to visit the school when they were invited to attend student performances and other special classroom events. At the end of the year, the seventy O'Hearn students went on a field trip to the downtown offices of the law firm, where they had lunch and were able to interact with their special pen pal. This was a tremendous experience for our students and a special treat for the lawyers and other staff.

The school and the students greatly benefited in having such an important ally when the O'Hearn was just starting inclusion. Goodwin, Procter & Hoar offered us some SEED funds for a second year and continued the pen-pal relationships for a few years after that. In many ways, GP&H helped catapult the O'Hearn into the limelight by bringing publicity to a partnership with a prestigious Boston business and by having an impact on a school that was trying to implement something that was then relatively innovative. As symbolized by the flowers and vegetables painted on the large mural near our school office, the SEED grant played a critical role in helping the O'Hearn grow and blossom into a beautiful, inclusive garden.

University Support: The Harvard Graduate School of Education Example

Over the years, the O'Hearn collaborated with approximately twenty universities located in the Boston area. Many staff members participated in courses and conferences offered at universities, and many university professors visited our school to conduct research, lead workshops, or provide technical assistance. Initially, the focus was primarily on learning how to teach students with disabilities. Subsequently, the focus shifted more on learning how to better serve students with diverse abilities in subjects like literacy, mathematics, science, social studies, and the arts.

The O'Hearn also received student teachers from approximately fifteen universities. Some of these interns participated in a full-time practicum for a semester, and some were part-time. Most of the experiences with interns were mutually positive, but early on, we learned that for a few student teachers, it was not a good fit. That's why I always told university coordinators that although I welcomed their interns, the individual interns from the university and teachers from the school needed to meet first and confirm that they wanted to work with each other. O'Hearn teachers needed interns who, the teachers felt, were comfortable with inclusion and pitching in and learning on the fly. Likewise, the interns needed supervising teachers who, the interns felt, could help them develop and learn appropriate skills.

As a result of our extensive collaboration with many universities, O'Hearn staff were better informed about effective instructional strategies. Teachers were able to refine and implement new techniques that proved beneficial for students with and without disabilities. Many O'Hearn staff were also invited by universities to share their expertise and practical experiences with others involved in education.

Our first collaboration with Harvard Graduate School of Education was with a project called Peace Games. In the late 1990s, Harvard students came to the O'Hearn and presented lessons in collaboration with our staff. Their program was designed to help students interact cooperatively, resolve problems effectively, and deal with anger constructively. Suggestions were also provided on ways to keep students engaged and active at recess. Teachers and parents appreciated the program. Although overall student behavior at the O'Hearn had not been a major problem, we found many Peace Game activities to be beneficial and incorporated them into our curricula.

A person who had a significant impact on the O'Hearn and on my work as principal was Tom Hehir. I first met Hehir, a strong advocate for youth and adults with disabilities, in the 1970s, when he worked for the Boston Public Schools. In 1993, President Clinton appointed Hehir director of the Office of Special Education Programs (OSEP). As director the following year, Hehir arranged for several key U.S. officials, including the secretary of education, Richard Riley, and assistant secretary of special education and rehabilitation services, Judy Heuman, to visit the O'Hearn and to observe inclusion in action. It was an honor for us to host top education leaders from our federal government. After the officials visited the classrooms, a group of O'Hearn staff and parents had a candid conversation with our guests about the importance and practicalities of inclusion. Secretary Riley was particularly moved to see and hear how students both with and without disabilities were learning at high levels in inclusive classrooms. Under the secretary's leadership, and with strong input from Hehir and Heuman, important national legislation supporting the rights of children with disabilities to participate in the general curricula with appropriate support and services was subsequently enacted.

When Hehir became a professor at Harvard in 2000, the O'Hearn developed a stronger partnership with the Harvard Graduate School of Education. Many O'Hearn teachers enrolled and participated in his dynamic classes. Most O'Hearn staff had opportunities to attend his talks or to read his articles or books. Not only did Hehir demonstrate a deep understanding of the practicalities of inclusion, but he also promoted programs and policies that supported it. As a strong friend and ally of the O'Hearn, he attended many special events at our school and advocated for programs and policies that supported us.

As part of their course work, students from Hehir's classes engaged in action research projects. In 2008, we welcomed six students from his class (two students were also O'Hearn staff) to help us determine the impact of Kurzweil, an assistive-technology company whose software package we used. As described in other chapters, the Kurzweil software was an accommodation that allowed students to both see and hear text, and it provided other tools to facilitate reading and writing. The researchers investigated the reading comprehension of fourteen O'Hearn students who had specific learning disabilities that affected their abilities to decode. The study found that all fourteen students' scores improved to varying degrees on standardized reading comprehension assessments when they were using Kurzweil; the average increase in reading level was 1.5 years.

Hehir was already supporting us in our efforts to promote accommodations for students with special needs. The research project conducted by his students affirmed and bolstered our belief in the importance of providing text-to-speech accommodations for students with print disabilities. O'Hearn students who needed and used Kurzweil programs regularly read more and at higher levels. They developed confidence and began to view themselves as successful readers. In addition, although very few of the O'Hearn's students with print disabilities had previously scored above the needs-improvement level on the state's English/language arts assessments, most scored at the proficient or advanced levels with the approved Kurzweil accommodation. First and foremost, their achievement was significant for themselves and their families. But beyond this benefit, the achievement demonstrated clearly how students with print disabilities could perform at rigorous levels and could even help raise a school's scores on the state's ranking index.

Hehir encouraged me to consider taking principal interns from the Harvard School Leadership Program. I had already welcomed principal interns from other universities. Frankly, there was always plenty to do, and being the only administrator at the school, I appreciated the opportunity to share and discuss some of the challenging issues with them. The interns were a great help for me and for the school as a whole. I certainly was not shy about sharing some of the numerous daily tasks, and the interns also assumed responsibility for many specific projects.

The Harvard principal interns came to the O'Hearn two or three days per week and participated in a full course load on the other days of the week. One area in which the interns helped me a great deal was data analysis. Although I understood and appreciated the value of analyzing student assessments and other data, the actual process of doing it, whether on paper or with alternative technology, was trickier for me as a blind person. In addition to helping me specifically, the interns sampled plenty of other leadership experiences common for all principals and gained much practical experience working in our urban inclusive school. They certainly had plenty to write about in their reports and journals. As a result of working with many interns, I participated in numerous forums and workshops coordinated by educators at Harvard. The insights and the collegiality provided by these opportunities were valuable to someone whose job by its very nature affords little chance for interactions with other principals.

In the summer of 2008, Tom Hehir introduced me to a Harvard graduate student, Tricia Lampron, who wanted to be a principal intern at the O'Hearn. Interestingly, Lampron lived close to the O'Hearn and had previously served as a teacher and teacher leader in a nearby elementary school. As a principal intern, Lampron quickly demonstrated her talents as well as a strong commitment to inclusion. She worked very hard with O'Hearn staff, parents, and students to help improve teaching and learning. After a long process, she was selected by the superintendent of Boston to be the next principal at the O'Hearn and started officially on July 1, 2009. It was wonderful for me to be able to pass on the baton, an honorary white cane, to someone who was so competent and experienced with our inclusive school.

10

·:·⟡·:·

HUMOR, LEVITY, AND GRACE

THE STUDENT'S CHALLENGE

"Let me go. Let me go! I'm going to kill him!"

These are the words that Steven was screaming while I was trying to restrain him from continuing a fight with a classmate. Steven and another boy had been pushing and hitting each other at recess. The lunch monitor who was supervising the class sent someone to the office to request my immediate assistance. I rushed outside to the courtyard. The other boy had stopped, but Steven was still enraged, so I was holding on to him.

I had witnessed Steven getting a little upset before, but never had he gotten that much out of control. Steven, a fifth-grader, was generally a cooperative kid and good student. He had significant problems with asthma and required regular treatments at home and at school, and he had been hospitalized a couple of times for it. His doctors had also recently informed the family that he was at risk for diabetes.

It took about ten more minutes for Steven to calm down enough before he could assure me that he was not going to try to fight anymore with the other student. I was relieved for my-self as well as for him. Steven was a hefty boy, measuring over five feet tall and weighing around 170 pounds. I escorted him to the office, where we both caught our breath and drank some water. I told Steven that I would be speaking with the other boy next, but that I wanted to hear his story first.

After calming down, Steven explained to me that he had "gotten so mad" because the other boy had taunted him with terrible words. He refused to repeat the exact words, because he said that he was not supposed to "say any swears." Steven's family was indeed very religious, and they attended church a few times a week. I tried to coax the swear word out of him by asking if it started with the letter *b*, *f*, or *a*. He told me that it was worse than those words and that he could not say it.

I left Steven in the office and went to his class to check with the boy who had fought with him. That boy admitted that he had yelled at Steven, but denied any swearing. He maintained, and Steven subsequently confirmed, that all he had repeatedly shouted was the cryptic phrase "your generation."

Name-calling was a recurring issue that we dealt with peri-odically at the O'Hearn. The general rule was that you didn't call anyone a name that was either inappropriate or something that the other person did not like. There were always some stu-dents testing this rule, and I usually handled it following a pro-gression of consequences, including warnings, written assign-ments, parent conferences, and, in serious or repeat situations, suspension hearings.

Fifth-grade students had recently been experimenting with a string of name-calling starting with the word "your" and fol-lowing it up with words like "mother," "sister," grandfather," and now, for the first time, "generation." The name-calling was not acceptable, but the fighting was an unwarranted response and clearly more serious.

Later that day, Steven and the other boy were able to talk things out and apologize to each other. They both had a good laugh once they understood how "your generation" was not offensive unless directed rudely at someone older, like me. Steven's parents came to school the next morning, and in front of them and Steven, I reiterated that fighting was dangerous and never acceptable and that he could be suspended from school if it happened again.

Steven's mother related that he was going through a very sensitive stage around his health complications and how a few kids had recently made fun of his bulky size. I assured her that we would monitor the situation, and I further explained what he, like other students at the O'Hearn, were supposed to do if teasing or name-calling occurred. He could ignore the kids, tell them to stop, speak with any staff member, come talk with me, or communicate with his parents—or do some combination of these—but he should not respond by calling names and he should never fight. We all stressed to him that fighting over something as foolish as hurtful words had even cost some young people their lives in the neighborhood. The parents agreed to check in with the teachers about Steven's work and behavior in a few more weeks.

As a consequence for his fighting that day on the playground, Steven was not allowed to participate with his class at recess for a week. Instead, he was assigned to assist a kindergarten class that had recess at the same time in another, smaller play area of the school. His job was to make sure that the kids used good language and played well together. Steven was a great help, and the little ones clearly looked up to him. He continued to help that class once in a while, even after his "punishment" was over.

Steven finished the rest of the school year without further incident. He passed all his tests, completed his work, and got along fine with the other kids. His teachers reviewed with the class how students could deal with teasing and name-calling at school, and they provided opportunities for role-playing and discussion about what to do with similar situations that often occurred in the neighborhoods. Steven still encountered a few instances of teasing that were somewhat problematic, but he dealt with them appropriately, following the options that we had described to him.

Upon leaving the O'Hearn, Steven went to a nearby middle school, where his behavior and work were both positive. Unfortunately, he continued to have significant problems with asthma and started to receive treatments for diabetes. When he was just fifteen years old, Steven had a serious asthma attack one night and died in his home. His parents were heartbroken and requested prayers and support. Many O'Hearn staff attended his funeral service, which was organized to be a celebration of his life. The church community was a great comfort to the family, but everyone clearly mourned the loss of such a young person to health complications.

THE PRINCIPAL'S CHALLENGE

Looking back, I have to admit that I experienced some anger around my vision loss. When I was younger, I sometimes felt mad at my parents. Retinitis pigmentosa (RP) was a genetic disease, and the doctors believed that both of my parents had been carriers even though there was no previous history of it on either side of the family. Two of my three brothers developed RP as adults (though none of our combined thirteen children have any symptoms). At any rate, it was hard for me to blame my parents for something about which they had no knowledge, and even if they had known, what else should they have done? To their credit, they always encouraged me to achieve and be positive. Sometimes I felt frustrated with God. Why had a caring God allowed me to go blind, and why had I not been cured despite many prayers? Of course, I recognized that there were far greater infirmities and far more suffering than RP and that God did not seem to intervene that frequently to alter those particular conditions, either.

The person whom I got angry with the most was myself. I hated the fact that I could not stop my vision loss. RP affects people differently, and with me, it was gradual. In my twenties, I lost much of my peripheral vision. In my thirties, I could not see details or regular print. In my forties, I stopped trying to magnify print and to distinguish people by sight. As I reached my fifties and am moving into my sixties, lights and bright colors were and are the only sure sights for me.

Ironically, my blindness bothered me emotionally the most when I was younger and when my vision was less impaired. There were times in my twenties and thirties when I became extremely frustrated, particularly when I couldn't find items that I had dropped or when I bumped into people or objects. If this occurred in public, I felt embarrassed. If it happened in my home, I sometimes felt like screaming or punching a wall. I had to learn how to accept the blindness that I could not change and to learn how to deal more effectively with it. I also needed to learn how to appreciate life and my many blessings. In some ways, it reminded me of swimming in a strong ocean current. You cannot fight directly against it, so you have to learn how to maneuver through it. I could not have been an effective principal if I had remained angry or depressed about going blind. I found that humor, levity, and grace were critical for me.

As a principal, I had to deal creatively and playfully with some embarrassing situations that arose due to my blindness. For example:

- When hustling around the school in crowded areas, I sometimes stepped on students' feet. If the student were someone with whom I knew that I could fool around, I would often say, "Why did you put your foot under my shoe?"
- Usually, I was successful in identifying staff members by their voices. I remember the time, though, when I greeted a young female teacher in front of others by calling her the name of the older male custodian. Her voice was a little hoarse that day, and she had sounded a little like him. But her shriek of protest at my mistake was at a much higher pitch!
- One day, I deliberately sat at a cafeteria table among a group of boys who needed some monitoring and modeling regarding their behaviors at lunch. Evidently, I must not have put my tray of lasagna and peas back far enough on the table, because when I sat down on the bench, I knocked all my food onto my lap. So when we finished laughing and cleaning up, I was the one to ask the boys to show me appropriate eating techniques.
- Large numbers of parents always attended the many student performances in our auditorium. Usually, I kept

moving around checking on things, but sometimes I sat down for a bit to enjoy the show. I located empty chairs by tapping them with my cane and by asking if anyone were sitting there. On a couple of occasions, when it was hard to hear because children were singing, I plopped onto the lap of a parent instead of an empty seat. I tried to graciously excuse myself, but often added—depending on the person—how much more comfortable it was sitting on her lap than on the metal chairs.

- Almost every day, I spent some time checking on what was happening at recess. Once in a while, a ball that a student had kicked hit me. I usually yelled loudly for that student to come over to me and pretended that he or she was in big trouble. When the offender approached me, however, I always whispered into the student's ear something like, "Don't worry, I'm fine. You've got a good, strong foot."

- One afternoon, I had just finished privately criticizing a teacher in her room (I never did this in front of others, of course) for not following my recent directive to escort her students all the way to the buses at dismissal. I thought that I was exiting her room but instead opened the door and stepped straight into her closet. She had a lot of fun on my account relating that story. After our meeting, however, her students did arrive at the buses in a much more orderly manner.

- Teachers regularly shared with me some of the challenges they were dealing with. On one unforgettable day, a teacher elaborated on a number of difficulties, so I put my hand on her shoulder and offered some words of support. She was quiet for a few moments, and I thought that she was pondering over my suggestions. Then she politely suggested, "Bill, how about taking your hand off my breast." I had thought my hand was on one of those puffy shoulder pads!

- There were many times when university folks came to the school to collect data or to interview me. On one occasion, the secretary announced that the researcher had arrived to ask me orally the questions on a long survey. I grumbled that I didn't really want to do that survey, that I didn't have the time to do it, and that I thought that the whole study was stupid. Then I asked the secretary to send the researcher into my office. The secretary quietly informed me that she had already entered and was sitting right in front of me. I apologized and proceeded to answer the questions in great detail.

- Parents frequently came to discuss various issues with me. One afternoon, a mother entered while I was just finishing eating an apple. After she was settled, I took a last bite and tossed what was left of it toward the spot where a small trash barrel was usually kept. Someone had moved it, though, and the half-eaten apple fell right into the parent's large, open bag. I offered to try to find the messy apple and clean the inside of the bag, but she smartly opted to minimize any additional damages and took care of it herself.

Everybody has to learn how to deal with embarrassing situations. Being blind, I have probably experienced more than my share of these. I could have chosen to avoid potential challenges by secluding myself more in the office or by protecting myself more with constant assistance. However, such isolation was not my style. Nor would such an attitude have been fair in a school with so many needs that required everyone to work hard and to pull his or her own weight. The scope of the work of a principal is all-encompassing, and the pace can be frenetic. Even though blindness only directly affected a relatively small percentage of the tasks that I encountered, it did force me to laugh at myself more and to be more flexible. Recognizing that total competence was a myth, I was better prepared to accept my own and others' missteps. Whatever our situations, we all need to find the strength and support to handle the best way we can whatever life throws at us, to move on, and to try to keep getting better.

IMPLICATIONS FOR THE SCHOOL

Disability, in and of itself, is not funny. Some of the conditions that O'Hearn children and their families faced were incredibly complex and challenging. There were, however, times in school when students with disabilities found themselves in situations that were indeed quite amusing. Appropriate humor was sometimes warranted and even proved beneficial. The ability to laugh at certain situations, or to respond with levity to them, helped sustain and enrich both staff and students. Consider these examples:

- A boy who had cerebral palsy and chronic digestive issues occasionally made loud noises passing gas. Although others were supposed to and usually did ignore this, it was great to hear how he chuckled after one of his buddies playfully shouted out, "What an explosion!"
- During a social studies presentation for students and their families, a student with intellectual disabilities

was asked to name the governor of Massachusetts. The student had prepared carefully, but, in her excitement, pointed at her mother and yelled, "Mommy!" After the audience settled down, the teacher asked the beaming student if she could identify the *second* most famous person in the state. She then correctly announced the governor's name.

- In response to a query from a visitor about how things were going, a student with Tourette's syndrome responded by blurting, "F——ing good." A classmate quickly interceded by explaining that the boy had one of those "swearing disabilities" and that the visitor should not pay attention to that word. Interestingly, that classmate eventually became a social worker who supported persons with mental illness.

- A large and clever student pushed a classmate aside to position himself in front of the line. Subsequently, in my office the culprit readily admitted having done the misdeed but announced to me and the other boy that he did not have to say that he was sorry, because he had autism and it was not in his nature to apologize. I stood up and asked him if I were to walk past him and accidentally step on his foot (he did not like physical contact), would I also be exempt from apologizing because I was blind? As I got closer to him, he quickly blurted out to the boy that he was indeed "very sorry."

- A boy who was fragile and used a wheelchair because he had very brittle bones, garnered a tremendous round of applause and a lot of laughter because he came out on stage dressed as a German soldier driving a tank during a scene from the school's performance of *The Sound of Music*.

- A girl using a communication device was supposed to hit the "Welcome to the O'Hearn" button to greet the visitors entering our school. Instead, she hit the button that said, "Will you take me to the bathroom, please?"

- A kindergarten boy with emotional disorders was accused by a classmate of calling her a "bad word." Upon persistent questioning, the boy argued vehemently that he had never called the girl anything really bad like "frog face," but instead had just called her a "b——."

- A teacher came to the office to proudly report that her student with Down syndrome had finally followed the rule of not taking food from other kids when eating lunch in the cafeteria. While the teacher was boasting about this, another student rushed into the office to announce that the same student had just emptied out and eaten the leftovers from eleven lunch boxes and bags that her classmates had put back in the classroom before going out for recess.

- Wearing a costume of satin and fur and with a great deal of dramatic flair, a student with limited speech and with intellectual disabilities elicited howls of delight from the packed audience for her dance rendition to a song recorded by Bessie Smith.

- A girl backing up in her electric wheelchair to position herself for a party knocked the entire tray of cupcakes onto the lap of the birthday boy. She gasped, but the boy made her feel better by pointing out that now he could eat more than his usual share of frosting.

- During a discussion about games that people play, a fifth-grade boy with cognitive delays shared with his class that his father liked to play with his mother in the bedroom before going outside to play with his cars.

All of these situations involved students with disabilities and elicited varying degrees of laughter. Students without disabilities at the O'Hearn certainly found themselves in plenty of amusing circumstances, also, but the examples above were definitely accentuated by disabilities. It was important for us at the O'Hearn to develop a culture in which all students and staff could laugh and have some fun with each other in a way that was supportive and not demeaning even when disabilities were involved. Some of this was subjective, because how individuals felt in response to the laughter varied tremendously. However, I believe that it is critical both for students with disabilities and for those without to become more comfortable with appropriate humor and teasing, whether the child is giving it or receiving it.

The key criterion is what is *appropriate*. Humiliating or bullying another child is obviously never appropriate. When this occurred at the O'Hearn, we dealt with it according to school rules and to Boston Public School procedures. The result was a range of disciplinary actions that included warnings, time-outs, loss of privileges, parent conferences, suspensions, referrals to a counseling and intervention center, and, in rare occasions, police involvement. However, compared with the statistics and anecdotes from other schools, such infractions happened less frequently at the O'Hearn and were seldom directed at the children who were the most vulnerable. If anything, including children with significant disabilities helped elicit interactions that were more kind and playful. Perhaps this occurred because students felt less of a need to compete or pretend to be perfect around children with complex challenges. I believe that interacting and having some fun with students who had significant disabilities provided opportunities for O'Hearn students to show more humanity and to learn how to relate more positively. It also helped them develop a clearer understanding of the words to use and the actions to take in situations when they felt that someone was being picked on or otherwise treated unfairly.

Teasing was another important issue, and in our initial years with inclusion, some staff and parents raised concerns about it. Some believed that it was always wrong to tease a student with a disability. I believed then—and still believe—that students with disabilities can benefit from learning how to both receive and give some teasing, as long as it is appropriate. In order to be appropriate, the teasing needs to be publicly acceptable and something that the person can handle. This definitely varies according to the time, place, and other circumstances as well as on the personality of the individuals. In my experience, students with and without disabilities who learned how to comfortably fool around with their peers seemed to be more socially competent and to be happier in school.

At the O'Hearn, we were committed to helping students develop general social skills in addition to helping them master the rigorous general curricula. This meant that we had to both model and teach appropriate humor and playing around. Developing this capacity was indeed trickier to do when we were involving students who had developmental or emotional impairments. For example, many students on the autism spectrum demonstrated awkwardness in social situations. We needed to guide some of these students both individually and in small groups about specific phrases that they could say or about actions that they could take to interact more comfortably with others. It was particularly important to help prepare some of these students for playful situations that occurred outside of classrooms, in places such as the school cafeteria, the playground, and even popular sites in the community.

Another social challenge was that many students with intellectual disabilities were easily swayed to follow the requests or behaviors of their peers. A boy who had Down syndrome and limited speech started uttering the *f*-word in class. Upon investigation, it turned out that some boys had taught him that word on the bus and that they had laughed every time he repeated it. He, of course, loved their perceived camaraderie and attention. We explained to his buddies that if the boy continued, he would get in trouble in school and at home and that it would hurt his chances of doing well and ultimately of ever getting a job. The boys were remorseful; they understood how important it was for them not to model bad words or to give positive reinforcement for them. We subsequently took advantage of their effective teaching skills by requesting that they help the boy learn more constructive words while riding with him on the bus.

Many students with emotional disorders had difficulties with conflicts or stress. We needed to spend extra time counseling them and demonstrated role-playing techniques or words that the children could use when they started to become agitated. Likewise, we reminded other students that it was wise not to antagonize others and particularly those who get overly upset.

It is human nature for students to sometimes try to fool teachers and parents about their work or behavior. Like other

educators, I sometimes needed to get a little creative and playful to extract the truth, as the following examples show:

- When checking on students who I suspected had not
  adequately completed their writing assignments, I usually requested that they start reading at the beginning of
  their paper or at the top of their computer screen. If the
  assignment was supposed to be long and I did not have
  time to hear all of it, I asked them to read the first couple of sentences of each paragraph. Unless they could
  keep reciting with fluency from the new locations, they
  admitted that they had much more to do. To help move
  them along, I then asked questions to make sure that
  they knew what they were supposed to do and that they
  had some specific ideas about what to write about next.
  Finally, I notified them that when I returned, I expected
  to see major improvements.
- When checking on students who we presumed were not
  keeping up with their reading, I asked them to tell me
  how many pages they had read. Then I asked some of the
  key comprehension questions that the teacher had highlighted. If I were not familiar with the story, I sometimes
  invented a character or situation and asked the student
  to elaborate on that. For those who fabricated responses,
  I congratulated them on their imagination, but informed
  them that I expected to hear from them later on regarding on what the author had written.
- When checking on students who we thought had either
  guessed at or had copied the answers in mathematics,
  I asked them to describe their work and the steps that

they took to solve the problems instead of just stating the answer.

- When checking on students who denied committing infractions like throwing objects, I reminded them that I would be easier on them if they told me the truth. I always reduced the consequences for those who were honest. However, if they did not accept responsibility, I then gathered information by talking with possible witnesses privately or by asking others to anonymously write down the names of those whom they had seen committing the infraction. With strong evidence, most children reluctantly admitted their guilt. However, I sometimes encountered hard-core deniers. They received the additional assignment of writing an essay for me describing how so many others who witnessed their transgressions could have been so deceived.

- I often checked on the condition of areas around the school to make sure that students had used them appropriately and had picked up after themselves. Usually, I did this by asking students to describe what they saw. Finding wet paper towels stuck to the walls happened periodically. With a student's guidance, I easily swept them down onto the floor with my cane and then, with the help of students, kicked them over to the corner. Next, I would investigate which students had just been in the bathroom. Sometimes, I tried to trick possible culprits by accusing them of throwing a hundred paper towels, and they, feeling unjustifiably accused, blurted out that that they had only thrown a couple of them. By instituting a rule that all students had to immediately report any problems in the bathrooms to their teachers or they could be considered accomplices, it became much easier to pinpoint the guilty ones, since the offenders were often the last ones to use the facilities without having reported a problem. Interestingly, some of the students were surprised that the principal interns who worked with me were able to see any errant paper towels.

Playful humor and levity were also helpful in my many interactions with staff and families. Teaching and parenting are often stressful, and working with students who have disabilities sometimes poses additional challenges. I often tried to make light of certain situations by telling what I hoped was a playful joke. Unfortunately, this did backfire on me sometimes, and I needed to learn to discern with whom and how much to fool around.

Nevertheless, the job was demanding and could be draining without a little fun, and as principal, I bore responsibility in setting a certain tone. Yes, I expected everyone to work hard, and yes, students and staff needed to perform at high levels, but I also hoped that all of us could, at the right moments, find enjoyment, too. Including children with significant disabilities helped remind us of the importance of taking delight in the students' daily efforts and growth. Celebrating accomplishments, both small and large, helped fortify us in our quest for continuous improvements and excellence for all O'Hearn children.

EPILOGUE

What is most important for any school is the accomplishments of its students. As I have pointed out throughout this book, not every child at the O'Hearn achieved as highly as the staff or parents desired. However, the overall performance of the students learning in our inclusive school was strong both academically and socially, and almost every child made significant improvements.

A majority of students with and without disabilities at the O'Hearn demonstrated high academic achievement on both state and district assessments, and the school as a whole was classified at the high average performing level. Those students who did not score at proficient levels usually made substantial progress toward proficiency, or if they had intellectual disabilities, they usually attained their alternate goals. Student work that was collected in portfolios or exhibited throughout the school generally showed creativity and rigor.

Over the years, many O'Hearn students received public honors and recognition. Examples of their writing and artwork were displayed throughout the community and published in the media. Students were featured on news broadcasts, documentaries, and other special programs. O'Hearn children performed and made presentations at many important community and school-wide events. The school received awards for accomplishments in inclusion, academics, arts, technology, and family involvement. All students were recognized at the school at various times throughout the year for their excellent work and contributions. Family and staff were proud of the children and their successes.

On June 23, 2009, a week before my official retirement from the Boston Public Schools, there was a special celebration in the O'Hearn courtyard. At this event, which had lots of media coverage, Mayor Thomas Menino and Superintendent Carol Johnson announced that the O'Hearn School was being renamed the Dr. William W. Henderson Inclusion Elementary School. Children from each of the classes presented a brief song, dance, poem, or speech during the ceremony. The whole event and the renaming of the school were very moving for me and left me feeling humbled and extremely grateful.

Less than two weeks after the school's renaming, I attended the annual convention of the National Federation of the Blind (NFB), which was held that year in Detroit. The NFB is the largest group representing the blind, and over two thousand members attended the meeting that year. At the convention, Marc Maurer, president of the NFB, and David Ticchi, a well-known blind educator from Massachusetts, presented me with the 2009 National Blind Educator of the Year award. It was a special tribute, and again, I was honored and humbled.

It is somewhat ironic that I received these and other awards for my work as a principal. My career as an educator could easily have ended early on. I clearly benefited from a confluence of circumstances as well as considerable support. When I started teaching in 1973, important national civil-rights legislation protecting disabled adults and children was just being enacted. Up until then, very few school systems even considered hiring individuals who were blind, and the schools were under no obligation to try to accommodate any existing teachers who started to lose his or her vision. During all those years when my vision gradually decreased, my family and friends were supportive, educators and colleagues were encouraging, blind persons helped me develop new skills and resiliency, and leaders within the Boston Public Schools gave me many opportunities. I was indeed most fortunate.

Despite these favorable circumstances and much support, I still had to work hard and keep learning. Continuous effort and learning were also what we expected of all our students, many of whom faced circumstances far more challenging than blindness. Throughout this book, I have provided examples of how my experiences dealing with blindness helped me to further develop qualities that made me a stronger principal:

- I became more determined to prove to others as well as to myself that individuals with disabilities could succeed.
- I experienced firsthand that there were different ways of learning and many paths toward success.
- I became more sensitive to the diversity of needs and to the importance of promoting high expectations.
- Going blind forced me to become more organized and efficient.
- Blindness made me to collaborate much more extensively with staff, parents, outside supporters, and the students.
- Being blind helped me learn to laugh at and move on from difficult situations more easily, as well as to better appreciate the joy of daily living.

There were some who questioned the use of the word *inclusion* in the new name of the school—the Dr. William W. Henderson Inclusion Elementary School. Some suggested that inclusion should be presumed for all students and should not have to be spelled out or articulated. Although I was not involved in drafting the new name of the school, I recognize that not having to state the word *inclusion* in the title of an organization would be the ideal. However, at the time of the writing of this book, inclusion in the United States was far from being an ordinary occurrence or the norm, and many individuals and groups are still struggling to realize it. I appreciate that the parent and teacher leaders of the O'Hearn requested that the word *inclusion* be incorporated into the new name of the school, as their goal was to remind people of the history of the struggle for inclusion and to ensure its continuance. I also considered it an honor to have the word *inclusion* associated with my name. If I had followed the advice recommended to me by some who were considered experts, I am well aware that the words describing my career in education could easily have been *exclusion* or *seclusion*.

Developing an effective, inclusive school was a team effort. It involved the school staff, families, outside supporters, and the students themselves. I was privileged to be the O'Hearn's leader, and I keenly recognize how so many contributed in so many ways. Those of us involved in the initial years of inclusive education were pioneers. When we started integrating students with disabilities, relatively few schools in the country welcomed and included students with some of the significant intellectual and developmental challenges affecting many of our children. The work was challenging, we didn't know exactly what we were supposed to do, and we were constantly trying to figure out how to do things better.

We quickly learned that inclusion could not exist in a vacuum and that strong general education needed to be its foundation. Ironically, the very process of including students with some of the most significant disabilities is what helped us transform the O'Hearn into a more effective school for everyone. That is why, in this book, I have focused more attention on students with special needs rather than on their nondisabled peers, who were the majority and who were indeed an essential part of the community. As I have tried to illustrate with specific examples throughout this book, working with the children who had disabilities became the catalyst that helped all the members of the O'Hearn community further develop qualities that improved teaching and learning for everybody.

I am deeply grateful for all the staff, family members, students, and outside supporters who worked so hard for inclusion at the O'Hearn. Although legislation and policies supporting inclusion were clearly important, it was the daily words and actions of many people—our champions of inclusion—that made it happen. I am also proud that the existing community, now called the Henderson Inclusion School, has continued the mission of providing high-quality, inclusive education. The journey toward excellence is clearly ongoing there. I am confident that the students at the Henderson Inclusion School will continue to learn and succeed and that the school will continue to shine.

ABOUT THE AUTHOR

Bill Henderson was an educator in the Boston Public Schools for thirty-six years. He started in 1973 as a middle-school teacher and later served as a staff trainer and curriculum developer before becoming an assistant principal at a K–8 school. In 1989, Bill was appointed principal of the Patrick O'Hearn Elementary School with a mandate to include students with significant disabilities, and he remained its leader for twenty years. The school gained widespread recognition for inclusion, academic progress, the arts, technology, and family involvement.

Bill earned a BA from Yale University, an MA from Goddard College, and an EdD from the University of Massachusetts at Amherst. Upon his retirement from the Boston Public Schools in June 2009, the O'Hearn was renamed the Dr. William W. Henderson Inclusion Elementary School. Bill continues to advocate for inclusion through consulting and by presenting at universities and conferences. He also enjoys spending time with friends and family, especially with his grandchildren.

Readers can contact Bill Henderson by e-mail at whenderson50@comcast.net.